THE
EDMONTON
OILERS

The Players, Games & Stories behind
Hockey's Legendary Team

Peter Boer

OVER
TIME
BOOKS

The Publisher: OverTime Books is an imprint of Éditions de la Montagne Verte

Library and Archives Canada Cataloguing in Publication

Boer, Peter, 1977-
    The Edmonton Oilers: the players, games & stories behind hockey's legendary team / Peter Boer.

ISBN-13: 978-1-897277-02-7
ISBN-10: 1-897277-02-4

1. Edmonton Oilers (Hockey team)—History. 2. Edmonton Oilers (Hockey team)—Biography. I. Title.

GV848.E35B64 2006   796.9626409712334   C2006-905302-2

Project Director: J. Alexander Poulton
Cover Image: Courtesy of Getty Images, photo by Don Smith

PC: P5

Contents

Dedication

For Aerya Rayne Mitchell
Born June 10, 2006

Acknowledgements

In all things hockey, my first thoughts are of Jay Poulton, even though he is first and foremost a Habs fan—thank you for this chance. To my mother, Faye, for her indefatigable patience and understanding. To my dad, Hank, for playing hockey with me when he didn't have to, and to my brother, Ryan, for pretending to like hockey, at least for a little while. Many thanks also to Derek and Tarra Mitchell for their awe-inspiring friendship, love and support over the last six months. And, of course, to the boys I spent most of May and June with, to Dan, Aly and Jamie, for sacrificing so many nights to cheer, cry and yell at the television screen during the Oilers' playoff run— they might not have won anything, but I did, in your friendship.

Introduction

November 22, 2003

The temperature in the city of Edmonton plunged into the high teens on an incredibly bright, sunny day, wrapping Alberta's capital in a frozen, winter blanket. And all 60,000 people crammed into Commonwealth Stadium could have cared less.

The city had been pulsing with excitement since tickets for the Heritage Hockey Classic first went on sale. The game would be an NHL first: a hockey game between the Montréal Canadiens and the Edmonton Oilers played outdoors, under the open sky. The evening game would be preceded by a classic showdown between alumni players of both clubs. Guy Lafleur, Steve Shutt and Larry Robinson would take the ice against Grant Fuhr, Jari Kurri and Paul Coffey.

And yes, Wayne Gretzky.

When he retired, "The Great One" stated publicly that he would never play in an "Oldtimers" game. When the Heritage Classic organizers contacted the Phoenix Coyotes owner, Gretzky recanted his statement, saying he would play just one game.

Tickets for the game became the most sought-after creature in the entire city. Would-be purchasers mailed in ballots and, if selected, were given the opportunity to purchase a certain number of tickets. Some bought for themselves, as well as friends and family. Others hawked their prizes on the Internet, where prices from hockey fanatics across North America soared into the thousands of dollars.

Construction of the rink itself began in earnest in early November 2003. Edmonton's icemakers, renowned for cooking up the best ice surface in the entire world, descended on the gridiron in northeast Edmonton, assembling boards, laying pipes and sand and watering down the whole mass until the ice was thick enough to paint. Working from a plan originally drafted in the summer, crews put the finishing touches on the rink within four hours of their forecasted target.

The Edmonton media had not seen an event worthy of such coverage since the Oilers last won the Stanley Cup in 1990, and they kicked into high gear. Special sections in the *Edmonton Sun* and *Edmonton Journal* regaled the city with Oilers trivia and history, resurrecting the careers of forgotten players, opining on the value of shinny hockey in Canadian society, and recalling the 1980 playoff series in which the fuzzy-cheeked, upstart Oilers steamrolled over hockey's most historic franchise.

While the city celebrated the event in the days leading up to the game itself, a fretful tension broke over Edmonton as thermometers began to drop. A cold air mass had swept through the city three days before, sucking the heat from the ground and pushing temperatures past the −20°C mark. The skies clouded over and opened up, dropping so much snow on the newly assembled ice surface that Zamboni crews had to make 52 runs to clear it. The media publicly worried, pressing organizers for a benchmark temperature at which the game might be called off.

Saturday, November 22, dawned cold, but it was still warmer than the days before. With 90 minutes to go until the alumni game began, fans clad in long underwear, layered sweaters and parkas descended unflinchingly on Commonwealth Stadium to take their seats. By noon, the temperature rose to −16°C, just inside the NHL's safety margin. The first game, it was announced, would proceed.

Those fans with seats at the highest point of the stadium sat exposed to winds breezing past at 10 kilometres per hour and squinted to see the rink built in the centre of the football field. Surrounded by an ocean of white tarp, the ice surface glistened in the afternoon sun as camera crews, staff and organizers scurried about, trying to make sure everything was in place before the puck dropped.

Although the alumni game was scheduled to go ahead, the actual NHL game between the Oilers and Canadiens was still in doubt. The sun was already disappearing behind the stadium bleachers when the Mega Stars game began. By the time both NHL teams took to the ice, the sun would be gone, taking precious degrees of warmth with it.

The crowd hummed excitedly as the clock counted down to faceoff time, then roared lustily when the public address announcer began introducing the players one at a time, alternating teams. Steven Penney and Richard Sevigny, known in history as the Canadiens goaltenders who came between Ken Dryden and Patrick Roy, would mind the pipes for *Les Glorieux*. Facing them would be two of Edmonton's three

Stanley Cup–winning goalies: Grant Fuhr and Bill Ranford.

Fans politely applauded and cheered for each Canadiens Mega Stars who took to the ice. These players, however, were not the Canadiens of its Cup-winning dynasty years. Shutt, Robinson and Guy Lapointe had been a part of the 1970s Cup-winning teams. Guy Carbonneau, Kirk Muller and Russ Courtnall had won the Stanley Cup with the Canadiens in 1993. Few in the crowd knew exactly what Gaston Gingras or Benoit Brunet had done.

Fans did, however, recognize Guy Lafleur and gave him the loudest ovation of all the Habs players when he was introduced. But the applause for Lafleur paled in comparison to the exponentially growing crescendo that greeted each Oilers alumnus. Ranford and Fuhr were each cheered, and serenaded louder still were Charlie Huddy, Paul Coffey and Dave Semenko. Glenn Anderson, Craig Simpson and Jari Kurri waved their sticks to the mob that thundered its approval with each introduction.

Had there been a roof on Commonwealth Stadium, Mark Messier's introduction would have blown it away. The six-time Cup winner and second-leading scorer in league history was the only active NHL player to take the ice. Captain of the New York Rangers, Messier's participation had been in doubt up until the bitter end when both he and Glen Sather chose to make the trip. There was one caveat: Messier would be one of only two skaters on the ice wearing a helmet.

The roar subsided, then exploded to a level heard only a few times before: in February 1989, when Edmonton hosted the All-Star Game; in October 1989 when the Los Angeles Kings came to town and the NHL crowned a new all-time scoring leader; and in 1999 when the Edmonton Oilers retired only the second jersey number in its history.

Wayne Gretzky paused in place as he was introduced as "The greatest player of all time," then walked to the rink, waving to the crowd. It had been 15 years since the trade that rocked the hockey world, but Edmonton fans had never forgotten Wayne. They celebrated his connection to the team and city every chance they could.

With Grant Fuhr and Steve Penney facing one another across the outdoor rink, referee Andy van Hellemond skated to centre ice and, to the delight of the crowd, dropped the puck. The Mega Stars game was on. Edmonton versus Montréal, two 15-minute periods before a titillated crowd of 60,000 fans.

Although the game had its vintage moments, it was not the high-scoring affair fans had been praying for. Fans roared their approval every time Gretzky got his stick on the puck and raced into the Montréal end. Grant Fuhr held his own at the Oilers end, turning aside repeated attempts by the Canadiens alumni to bulge the twine. Passes in the 1980s that would have found their mark were missed or ended up in the skates of the opposing players. There was little physical play as players steered clear of one another in the open ice and along the boards. Kevin Lowe accidentally cut in front of a Canadiens player, ran into him and immediately apologized. Former Oilers tough guy Jeff Beukeboom took to the ice, like Messier, wearing a helmet because of all of the concussions he had endured in his career.

Gretzky, playing with his jersey classically tucked into one hip, didn't score. His former linemate Jari Kurri didn't score. Glenn Anderson didn't score. Paul Coffey, the second-highest scoring defenceman of all time, didn't score.

No, the first Oilers goal went to a player whose time with the team in the 1980s was brief. With 1:38 remaining in the first half of the game, Ken "The Rat" Linseman, who took to the ice wearing sports goggles seen only on squash courts, got open in front of the net. Craig Simpson—known along with former Canucks coach Marc Crawford and referee Kerry Fraser for having the most perfect hair in hockey—fed the Rat a perfect pass from the boards. Linseman pulled the trigger and, to the delight of the crowd, scored the first goal.

The players weren't the only ones at fault for the slow, beleaguered style of play. The frigid arctic air was having an effect on both the ice and the puck. As both surfaces became colder, they also became harder. The puck skittered and twitched on its end, bouncing off the ice and over the sticks of would-be goal scorers. The only players the cold didn't seem to affect were Fuhr and Penney.

"It's a little chippy out there," Glen "Slats" Sather was heard to remark on the sidelines to his team. "Maybe some of you guys are too heavy."

Sather leaned into former Oilers enforcer Dave Hunter, whose expanding waistline since his retirement had made him the butt of repeated jokes by his teammates in the local media.

"Hunts, skate a little lighter. The ice is too chippy," Sather quipped. "We're going to have to short-shift you, David."

Much had been made in the local media of the Heritage Classic's connection to pond hockey, or shinny. Columnists in both Edmonton papers waxed eloquently about the simple beauty and majesty of Canada's small-town winter pastime. The players nodded and smiled when asked about the Mega Stars game's resemblance to games of pick-up. They fondly recalled evenings and weekends spent tuckering and tilting back and forth across a frozen lake or pond, honing their skills and creativity.

Yet despite the media hype, the Mega Stars game bore little resemblance to a true game of shinny. The fans watching were, of course, the first notable exception. This game was being played on an actual rink with actual boards and Plexiglas panels, whereas traditional games of shinny are surrounded only by banks of snow. The Mega Stars had proper equipment and matching jerseys, but on a pond in the middle of Saskatchewan, one can often see skaters wearing Microns and winter jackets. The Mega Stars game played five skaters to a side, plus the goalie, with referees, whereas most outdoor games involved 15 to 20 skaters at a time, often with no goalie, each man governed only by the universal "no slapshot, no body contact" rule.

There were no cars surrounding the rink to light up the ice when the sun fell. No players took a shift off to smoke a cigarette. And though the Mega Stars game was being played outdoors, it was not a classic outdoor game—until the first period ended.

With only a brief intermission between halves, most members of each team rested along the boards, chatting with old teammates and rivals.

But a select few players from each squad reached over the bench, grabbed a snow shovel, and began scraping snow and frost from the ice's surface. Like clearing an Alberta pond after a heavy snowfall so the neighbourhood kids could play, these former superstars took turns skating from one side of the rink to the other, scraping as they went, tossing mounds of snow over the glass or shoving it against the boards.

That was classic.

Both teams changed goalies but did not change ends. Bill Ranford stepped into the Oilers' crease, while Richard Sevigny skated to the Canadiens end. With one period behind them, both teams began to loosen up a little. Canadiens forward Russ Courtnall rubbed Hunter into the boards, then grabbed onto his waist and dragged him to the ice. Former super-pest Esa Tikkanen zeroed in on a Habs defenceman in the corner and skated full tilt towards him, leaping into the boards with a resounding crash, only brushing the player he had playfully targeted.

Bill Ranford carried Fuhr's shutout into the second period, repeatedly robbing the Canadiens players who managed to get in close. The Oilers lineup boasted no less than five 40-goal scorers, but it was a player who barely scored 100 in his entire career who proved to be the most potent offensive weapon. Defenceman and bruiser

Marty McSorley, who had followed Gretzky to L.A. in "the trade," managed to make three shots through the first 20 minutes of the game. At 9:39 of the second period, McSorley took a pass from the Rat and banked it off of a sprawling Sevigny into the net. It was 2–0 Edmonton.

And that's the way the first game ended. In just 30 minutes of hockey, two of the greatest teams in league history managed a grand total of 35 shots and 2 goals.

"That's Oilers hockey," Messier shouted as he hugged his former teammates at the end of the game. "That's Oilers hockey."

The night, however, was still young, and there was still more hockey to play. Halfway through the Mega Stars game, CBC announcer Chris Cuthbert announced to the televised audience that the evening game between the Oilers and Canadiens would proceed despite the weather.

The Zamboni scraped the ice. The sun fell and the temperature ploughed through −19°C. Each active player with the Oilers and Canadiens took to the ice sporting neoprene full-body underwear under their equipment. Canadiens goalie Jose Theodore took a step towards both warmth and heritage by stretching a Canadiens toque, complete with a pompom, over top of his goalie mask.

Buoyed as they were to be participating in such a spectacle, the Oilers could not seize the momentum of the day. After a scoreless first period, the Canadiens Richard Zednik struck first, redirecting a cross-crease pass behind Ty Conklin. Yanic Perreault capitalized on a powerplay to give the Habs a 2–0 lead before Oilers defenceman Eric Brewer buried a shot past Theodore to trim the Canadiens lead to one. The teams traded goals for the rest of the game as Perreault got his second on a wraparound, which was countered by a Jarrett Stoll goal off a Steve Staios rebound. Zednik scored his second on a breakaway to put the Habs up 4–2, until Staios hammered home a slapper from the point.

It was all the Oilers could muster. Although the Mega Stars before them had salted away a 2–0 victory, it was the Canadiens regulars who claimed a 4–3 win in the game that counted statistically.

The event was a watershed game for the Oilers. It gave both the team and the fans the chance to celebrate Edmonton's storied hockey history one last time, in a setting never before seen in the NHL. It was a chance to celebrate the glorious Stanley Cup runs of the past and the great hockey heroes responsible for them. In the last 13 years, the Heritage Hockey Classic was the crowning moment of the franchise.

That is, until 2006.

Chapter One

The Beginning

None of the owners in the NHL were taking them seriously.

The World Hockey Association (WHA) was offering a professional level of hockey with salaries that could often rival, if not exceed, what each player could make under the restrictive rules of the NHL's team owners. They were expanding into previously untested waters in Ottawa, Edmonton, Calgary and Winnipeg, few of which had arenas large enough to accommodate the anticipated number of fans. It would be only a matter of a year or two before the league folded outright, its critics thought.

The players, however, felt otherwise. Since the WHA allowed players as young as 18 to play, many of those young skaters decided to make the leap into the WHA instead of toil for an NHL farm team. More frightening still for the NHL, key players started making the jump from the NHL to the

WHA, as did Bernie Parent and Gerry Cheevers. The biggest of the fish to jump out of the NHL pool was Bobby Hull, who was lured north of the border to the upstart Winnipeg Jets for a 10-year, $2.75 million contract

The WHA had been the brainchild of two men in the U.S. who knew little about hockey. They did know basketball, though, having started up the short-lived American Basketball Association, which had made an impressive run before the NBA swallowed up some of its teams. Now the two men needed help getting their idea of the WHA off the ground. The answer was Bill Hunter.

An Edmonton businessman, Bill Hunter had always been surrounded by hockey. He'd been heavily involved with the Edmonton Oil Kings of the 1960s when they played out of the old Edmonton Gardens. Besides offering his advice on how to successfully run the WHA, Hunter also decided to start up his own franchise in Edmonton, the capital city of Alberta. He became one of the WHA's most fervent boosters, often "calling press conferences to announce press conferences," to announce some new development with respect to the team or league.

The Calgary franchise, however, pulled up its stake before the WHA's inaugural season, fleeing instead to Cleveland to play as the Crusaders. With only one WHA team in Alberta, Hunter decided to capitalize on the marketing potential, dubbing his new WHA franchise the Alberta Oilers. The team that took to the ice in its first 1972–73 season was a motley collection of old Oil Kings and young players who had bolted to the WHA instead of waiting to enter the NHL amateur draft. The Alberta Oilers opening lineup in 1972–73 featured many of "Billy's Boys," such as Dennis Kession, Eddie Joyal, Bob Wall and Al Hamilton.

"If it hadn't been for the WHA, there would be no Coliseum, no Edmonton Oilers in the National Hockey League and no Stanley Cups in Edmonton," Hunter said later.

Playing out of the 5700-seat Edmonton Gardens, the Alberta Oilers struggled to a 38–37–3 record, finishing fourth in the WHA's Western Conference and squeaking into the playoffs with one of the last seeds. Their playoff run, however, was short-lived; they dropped their one-game playoff to the Minnesota Fighting Saints 4–2.

In spite of their record, the first season was not without its share of successes. Jim Harrison led the Oilers in scoring with a respectable 37 goals and 47 assists, while goaltender Jack Norris posted a decent 3.06 goals against average (GAA) in a league where games were more often offensive slug-fests than defensive trappings. Heading into their second season, the now renamed Edmonton Oilers were looking to improve on their first season's record.

That didn't happen. Head coach Ray Kinas-ewich was fired halfway through the inaugural season after a woeful start, and Bill Hunter took over the coaching reigns himself. The Oilers started Brian Shaw behind the bench for their second season, but he couldn't summon more from his players than they'd given the previous season. The second year was a repeat of the first, right down to the team's 38–37–3 record and their first round elimination at the hands of the Minnesota Fighting Saints.

At the end of their second season came good news for both the team and the city. The city of Edmonton council of the day agreed to build a brand new, major-league event arena that would, at its peak, hold approximately 17,000 fans. The WHA Oilers would be the rink's first major tenants, and everyone in Edmonton knew the capital city was aiming high for the arena's future: Edmonton wanted an NHL club.

Northlands Coliseum opened its doors to the public and the WHA on November 10, 1974. Although the fans came out to watch, the 1974–75 Oilers had problems showing up to play. The team now featured former Montréal Canadiens goaltending legend Jacques Plante between the pipes, but Edmonton still finished with a losing 36–38–4 record. And despite having University of Alberta Golden Bears coaching great Clare Drake behind the bench, Edmonton fared no better in the 1975–76 season, stumbling to a 27–49–5 record and losing their first playoff round to the Winnipeg Jets in four straight games.

The fact that the Oilers made the playoffs with such a pathetic record was proof that the WHA was no longer working. Teams were hopping from one city to another or folding outright, sometimes before they'd even started to play. The Toronto Toros lost $2 million, the San Diego Mariners $1 million, and Calgary, who had experienced a brief resurgence, posted $500,000 in losses. The Oilers were now one of the WHA's most stable franchises. The stability of the WHA, however, was entirely in doubt.

Having succeeded in his bid to bring hockey to Edmonton, Hunter decided it was time to take his leave from the professional hockey scene. In the 1976–77 season, the Oilers underwent a rapid ownership change in which the team changed hands three times. Hunter sold the team to Edmonton doctor and real estate owner Dr. Cam Allard, who quickly flipped the team to Nelson Skalbania, a BC businessman whose specialty was turning over properties for sale as quickly as he bought them. Being the owner of a major sporting franchise required planning and patience—two traits that were not Skalbania's strengths. After paying Allard $300,000 for the rights to the Oilers, Skalbania quickly turned to his good friend Peter Pocklington for help.

Pocklington epitomized the flare and substance of a high-wheeling businessman. Peter "the Puck" owned a Ford dealership in Edmonton, as well as numerous real estate holdings in Phoenix. He also dabbled in agribusiness, natural resources and financial services. He was both careful and fast with his money, leaping at any project with potential. His deals were sometimes impulsive, but to date he has been one of Edmonton's most successful businessmen. And he was interested in the Oilers.

During a late-night meeting at an Edmonton steakhouse, Skalbania and Pocklington crafted a deal the likes of which are seldom seen in the world of business. In exchange for half of the Oilers and half of the team's $1.6 million debt, Pocklington gave Skalbania a Rolls Royce, a painting and a diamond ring his wife happened to be wearing that night. All together, the deal was worth approximately $700,000.

The Oilers were now in the hands of two successful businessmen, while the rest of the WHA was hemorrhaging money and teams. Teams in Chicago, Baltimore and Minnesota folded in 1975 and 1976. Vancouver moved to Calgary; Denver moved to Ottawa, which had already lost one WHA team; and the Cleveland Crusaders contemplated a move to fill the void left in Minnesota.

All the Oilers could do was continue to play hockey and pray that the NHL would start showing more interest in subsuming their team. Neither, however, seemed to be happening. The Oilers were barely scraping along in the 1976–77 season and seemed doomed to miss the playoffs for the first time in their history. Armand Guidolin was axed as coach after the first 63 games as the Oilers stood on the edge of playoff ruin with a 25–36–2 record with 18 games remaining. Management was looking for a sacrificial lamb, and they seemed to have found it in Glen Sather.

Sather had been one of Billy's Boys, a captain with the Oil Kings in 1962–63 who eventually went on to play two seasons for the Boston Bruins. He was claimed by the Pittsburgh Penguins in the 1970 expansion draft and was traded to the New York Rangers in 1971. In 1973 he was traded to the St. Louis Blues, where he potted 44 points in 69 games. In 1974 he was traded to the Canadiens, who then traded him to the Minnesota North Stars in 1975. With his career winding down and his playing time dwindling, Sather decided it was time to find a team with which he could play out his career. The Edmonton Oilers seemed like the perfect team for that.

With 18 games left in the season and the Oilers needing a sustained effort to make the playoffs, Sather took over the helm of the team as player and coach for the final sprint to the finish. But there was little doubt that Sather's coaching career would last. As soon as the season was over and the Oilers were out of the playoffs, it was widely speculated he would be pushed aside as coach and quietly retire.

But Edmonton responded to Sather's on-ice coaching, posting nine wins and two ties in their remaining 18 games to make the playoffs. The post-season had never been the Oilers' strength and that curse continued as the Houston Aeros beat Edmonton in the first round. The Oilers' showing, though, was good enough for Peter Pocklington to make Sather the full-time coach. Sather dutifully hung up his skates and took his place behind the bench for the next season.

The 1977–78 season signalled the beginning of the WHA's death march into the history books. They were now down to a meagre pool of eight teams that could not possibly hope to sustain an entire league on their own. The WHA looked desperately to its NHL counterparts, who grudgingly entered into talks about maybe bringing some of the stronger WHA franchises into the NHL fold.

The end of the 1978 season would also see Edmonton's hockey saviour begin to stir the WHA pot.

Almost every hockey-loving Canadian knows the story of Wayne Gretzky. Born in Brantford, Ontario, Gretzky grew up under the tutelage of his father, Walter, who flooded the family's backyard every winter so young Wayne could practise his burgeoning hockey skills. The extra effort paid off, because Wayne was soon playing with 10-year-olds when he was five. In 1971–72, the 11-year-old scored a jaw-dropping 290 goals in minor hockey play.

His rise through the ranks of minor pro hockey was swift and sure. He was drafted by the Sault Ste. Marie Greyhounds in 1977, where he first started wearing his trademark jersey number 99. He scored 70 goals and 182 points, before adding 8 goals and 17 assists in six games at the World Junior Hockey Championships.

His size and stature, however, were cause for criticism in the NHL. His raw talent could not be denied, but the 17-year-old's 5' 10" height led many NHL scouts to believe the young phenom would not be able to withstand the physical rigours of professional hockey. Nelson Skalbania felt otherwise.

The one-time Oilers owner was not yet soured on professional hockey, having purchased a stake in the WHA's Indianapolis Racers for the cost of one dollar. Skalbania knew all about the Brantford hockey sensation, who was still a few years from being eligible for the NHL amateur draft. Skalbania decided his flailing organization needed someone with Gretzky's skill and raw talent and flew the Gretzky family to Vancouver to discuss a contract. The now-established legend goes that Skalbania, an active runner, took Wayne on a six-mile run that barely fazed the 17-year-old. As soon as they returned to Skalbania's home, the owner offered Gretzky a four-year contract that would pay him $1.125 million. The contract, however, was not with the team but with Skalbania personally. It gave the real estate mogul the right to effectively do whatever he wanted with Gretzky.

"He asked me, 'Do you think you can play pro hockey?' I told him, 'If I didn't think I could, I wouldn't be here,'" Gretzky later recalled.

Wayne's stay in Indianapolis—and that of the Racers—was remarkably short-lived. Needing crowds of at least 11,800 at his team's games to break even, Skalbania instead saw a mere average of 8000 fans watch his newest acquisition play. Gretzky still managed three goals and three assists in eight games, but his Racers career was effectively finished, as was the team.

Skalbania had one high-priced ace up his sleeve—Wayne Gretzky—and one long-time friend who was trying desperately to get his own team into the NHL—Peter Pocklington.

Pocklington also believed in the young Gretzky's potential and was prepared to sacrifice money for talent. In a straight-cash deal, Pocklington paid $300,000 for the rights to Gretzky as well as those of goaltender Eddie Mio and right winger Pete Driscoll. Mio had originally been drafted by the Leafs but spent most of his playing career in the WHA with Calgary, Québec and Indianapolis before being sold to Pocklington. Mio was a draft pick of the Chicago Blackhawks who toiled in Calgary, Vancouver and Birmingham before his NHL rights were traded to Minnesota.

The deal was a two-part trade in which Pocklington pledged to pay Skalbania another $550,000 if the Oilers were accepted to the NHL, which was beginning to look increasingly possible. In March 1978, the NHL reached an agreement with the WHA that would see teams in Edmonton, Winnipeg, Québec and Harford admitted to the NHL. The terms of the draft agreement, however, were draconian. Each team would have to pay $6 million for entry to the NHL, plus another $1.5 million to Cincinnati and Birmingham, the two remaining WHA teams not being admitted to the NHL. All of the NHL teams would be able to reclaim the players to which they held rights who were playing in the WHA, except for two goalies and two skaters. Wayne Gretzky and Gordie Howe, who was playing with Hartford, were also ineligible for the reclamation draft.

The NHL's Board of Governors, made up of the owners of all of the NHL teams, at first voted down the idea. One month later a second meeting was convened in which Vancouver and Montréal switched their votes, giving the draft agreement enough votes to pass. Starting in 1978–79, the Edmonton Oilers would play in the NHL.

With their future as a hockey city and team now secure, the Edmonton Oilers went on a tear in their last WHA season. The young Gretzky led the Oilers in scoring, potting 46 goals and 64 assists in his first full year in the WHA. His debut was so impressive that on January 26, Gretzky's 18th birthday, Pocklington signed the youngster to a new contract valued at approximately $5 million, which would keep Wayne in Edmonton until 1999. Wayne signed the contract at centre ice before a game against the Cincinnati Stingers, and then cut his birthday cake.

"Looks like I'm here for life," he said at the time.

With Eddie Mio backstopping the Oilers in goal, Edmonton actually made it past the first round of the playoffs and made it all the way to the league championship, the Avco Cup finals. In the end it was the Winnipeg Jets that came out on top, going down in history as the last WHA champions in the history of the league. No sooner had the final ended than the WHA ceased operations, closing what had been a daring and ultimately unsuccessful chapter in the history of professional hockey.

The summer that followed was one of frenzied activity as a series of drafts ensued to prepare the four new teams as well as the 17 current teams for the newly expanded NHL. Two dispersal drafts were held, the first redistributing players from Cincinnati and Birmingham to the four expansion teams. In the second draft, the NHL teams that owned the rights to players playing with the four expansion teams were permitted to reclaim those players and assign them wherever they wished. If a team could not fit a player onto their roster, the expansion team could pay the parent club $100 to keep their rights.

Once the dispersal draft gutted the four expansion teams, the NHL held an expansion draft in which Edmonton, Winnipeg, Québec and Hartford were allowed to select players from the current NHL teams. The pickings, however, were slim. The terms of the merger agreement specified that the NHL teams could protect two goalies and 15 skaters, more than three-quarters of a standard NHL roster. In total there were 761 players available.

"After pouring over the names, only 53 excited us a little. Too many of the players have huge, out-of-sight contracts, problems with their present coach or GM, a drinking problem or are already retired, like Bobby Orr. And that doesn't include the guys who aren't very good, period," said the Oilers' newly minted GM Glen Sather.

The Edmonton Oilers lost 12 players in the reclamation draft, including goaltenders Eddie Mio and Dave Dryden, as well as enforcers Dave Semenko and Dave Hunter. Semenko had been picked up during the 1977–78 season and scored 36 points while accumulating 298 penalty minutes. He was reclaimed by Minnesota, who held his NHL rights.

The expansion draft proved to be a bit of a bust for the Oilers. Before the draft began, Sather made a deal to acquire Dave Lumley and Dan Newman. He also managed to retrieve Mio and Dryden and hung onto Oilers veteran Al Hamilton during the reclamation draft. In the first round of the expansion draft, Sather selected Cam Connor from Montréal, then Tom Edur, a Pittsburgh defenceman. Tom Edur, however, had retired in protest of the growing violence of the game. Sather also took Inge Hammarstrom, who had returned to his native Sweden and vowed never to return to the NHL (and he never did), as well as Wayne Bianchin, a left winger who was recovering from spinal surgery and didn't know if he'd play in the NHL again (he played 11 games for the Oilers before retiring). Sather also selected former Saskatoon Blades all-star Pat Price from the New York Islanders. More noteworthy, however, was the selection of Buffalo Sabres defenceman Lee Fogolin, who had been a first-round selection in 1974. The addition of defenceman Doug Hicks from the Chicago Blackhawks rounded out what had been an almost useless draft.

Sather continued pulling back the players he'd lost in the reclamation draft, grabbing Stan Weir off waivers, trading for Risto Siltanen, and giving up two draft choices for Dave Semenko.

The new Oilers roster was a motley collection of the old, the indignant and the injured. If the Oilers were going to stand any chance of succeeding in the NHL, they would have to bolster their lineup with a succession of young players with solid skills. The chances of that happening in the upcoming entry draft, in which the Oilers were scheduled to pick last, appeared slim.

Chapter Two

Baby Steps

Glen Sather knew he had to pick well at the 1979 entry draft. His was not a position of strength: he was picking last of all the teams and had already surrendered his second round selections to get Dave Semenko back from the North Stars. He would have to look deep into the talent pool to find anyone capable of rounding out his team in Edmonton.

"It's obvious. We've got half a team here. We're going to find the other half in the next two or three years," said Pocklington.

Fortunately, the 1979 draft was deep in youth and talent. Ray Bourque, Mike Gartner, Michel Goulet, Rick Vaive and Rob Ramage were available and snapped up early, with Ramage going first overall. By the time the Oilers' 21st pick came along, Sather had decided on his man. With future standouts such as goaltender Pelle Lindbergh and winger Mats Naslund still available, Sather instead decided to stay in Canada and select, as the Oilers' first-ever draft pick, a defenceman named Kevin Lowe. The captain of the Québec Ramparts had grown up on his parents' dairy farm in Lachute, Québec. The levelheaded defenseman had scored a noteworthy 86 points in 68 games the previous season.

With no pick in the second round, the Oilers were forced to wait until the third round to make their next selection. Sather honed in on a local boy who had re-entered the amateur draft after a short stint in the WHA, a former member of the St. Albert Saints named Mark Messier. Messier came from good stock—his father Doug had played with the Edmonton Flyers in the 1960s.

Sather scored another coup in the fourth round, laying claim to winger Glenn Anderson, who was playing at Denver University and had racked up 55 points in 40 games south of the border. He was tall, agile and could skate with blinding speed.

The fifth and sixth selections were less remarkable as the Edmonton Oilers selected Maxwell Kostovich with their 84th pick and Mike Toal with their 105th. Neither would factor into the Oilers' future plans.

The immediate future was quickly dawning on the Oilers. Both Messier and Lowe won starting jobs in training camp, and the Edmonton team that took to the ice on October 10, 1979, though young, was brimming with talent.

"The whole thing about this year is to gain experience. To develop character as a team," said Gretzky. "If we don't make the playoffs, we'll go to camp and we'll be starting all over again. But if we do make the playoffs, we'd go into our future with a winning attitude. That's what we need. That attitude is everything. A lot is riding on this."

The issue of leadership raised its head in the local media. *Edmonton Journal* columnist Jim Matheson decried the "fuzzy-cheeked" ensemble that would play in the Oilers' inaugural season, while *Sun* writer Terry Jones declared in no uncertain terms that Edmonton would miss the playoffs. If they didn't, Jones declared, he would eat his column with a mixture of "bitter lemon, sour grapes and sauerkraut topped with sour cream."

The Edmonton Oilers played their first game against the Chicago Blackhawks at the venerable Chicago Stadium on October 10, 1979. In a story that none of the media could have written any better, it fell to the Oilers' first draft selection, Kevin Lowe, to score the team's first goal. With Edmonton on the power play, Lowe managed to sneak a backhand shot past Chicago Blackhawks legendary goaltender Tony Esposito.

Gretzky assisted on the play. Despite one other marker in the game, the Oilers couldn't keep up with the Hawks and ultimately dropped their first game 4–2.

The home crowds were healthy, with an average of 15,500 fans turning out for every home game. By January 1980, though, the Oilers were floundering noticeably. The team had the third-worst record in the league. Dave Dryden, the younger brother of Canadiens great, Ken Dryden, was struggling in net, and Eddie Mio was eventually forced to take over as starting goaltender. At the annual trade deadline, Sather traded perennial Oiler Ron Chipperfield to Québec for goaltender Ron Low then flipped expansion draft selection Cam Connor to the Rangers for forward Don Murdoch.

Sather was hoping Murdoch would be able to rediscover his scoring form, but the young forward's history was cause for concern. After a stellar rookie year in 1976 for the Rangers in which Murdoch scored 32 goals, the young forward fell into the trappings of fame and began using cocaine. After a sophomore season abbreviated due to injuries, Murdoch was arrested trying to board a plane in New York with 4.5 grams of cocaine stuffed into his sock. Murdoch was fined $400 and served a one-year suspended sentence. NHL president John Ziegler suspended him for the entire 1978 season but later lifted the suspension after 40 games. Murdoch never regained his form and soon became trade bait. His stint in Edmonton, though meant as a second chance, was brief.

The Oilers finished the season with a record of 28–39–13. In their final game of the season, facing off against the Colorado Rockies, Edmonton absolutely had to win in order to make the playoffs. Down 2–0, the Oilers managed to rally and win the game, propelling them into the playoffs—no small achievement for a first-year expansion team.

Terry Jones proved true to his word. He hunkered down with a shredded copy of his column doused in every unsavoury topping he had mentioned in his earlier column and, in front of his press colleagues, devoured every last piece.

Although significant for the team, the final standings for the year meant the Oilers would take on the Philadelphia Flyers in the first round. The Flyers had finished with almost 50 more points than the Oilers and had set the league record that year for going on a 35-game unbeaten streak.

"We might as well play the best team," said Ron Low. "And who knows, the way we're going now and with a short, best-of-five series...well, who knows?"

The Flyers knew. The Oilers twice took the Flyers to overtime in the first round series, but Philadelphia won all three games necessary to take the series. Whereas the Oilers bowed out of the playoffs early, the New York Islanders went on a tear, winning their first-ever Stanley Cup.

The highlight of the Oilers' inaugural season was definitely the performance of Wayne Gretzky. The Brantford kid who had been decried as being too little and too skinny to succeed in the NHL finished the season tied for the league lead in scoring with Marcel Dionne of the Los Angeles Kings, both finishing with 137 points. Dionne was awarded the Art Ross trophy as the league's highest scorer, having scored 53 goals to Gretzky's 51. Although his performance was by far the best of any of the NHL's first-year players, Gretzky was ruled ineligible for the Calder trophy, awarded to the NHL's best rookie, because of his season spent in the WHA. The WHA had been a professional league, the NHL ruled, so Wayne was no longer a hockey rookie.

Gretzky did take home the NHL's most coveted personal award, the Hart trophy, given to the league's most valuable player. He also won the Lady Byng award as the league's most gentlemanly player.

The Oilers' first season was a success, and a good showing in the 1980 amateur draft would definitely guarantee even more success in the years to come. With a vastly improved draft position, now picking sixth overall in the first round, Sather laid claim to a speedy, offensively gifted defenceman from the Kitchener Rangers named Paul Coffey. The long-haired, lanky kid had scored 102 points with the Rangers the previous season, a stellar offensive display from a blueliner.

The Oilers again had no selection in the second round and didn't impress in the third when they picked right winger Shawn Babcock, who never made it to the NHL. In the fourth round, though, Sather again struck gold in a location where no one was looking. Slats and the Oilers coaching staff saw in Jari Kurri, a right winger playing for Jokerit Helsinki in the Finnish Elite League, a solid, fast winger who might make a good addition to Gretzky's line. The fifth and sixth selections—left winger Walt Poddubny and centre Mike Winther—never factored into their future plans. It was the team's seventh round selection, a BC boy named Andy Moog who minded the net for the Billings Bighorns in the WHL that would help shore up the team's shortcomings in goal.

The Oilers team that took to the ice to start the 1980–81 season looked a little different from their previous season. Glenn Anderson had played an impressive year with the Canadian National Team program and was subsequently promoted to the big team during training camp. Jari Kurri overcame his initial reluctance to cross the Atlantic Ocean and agreed to give the NHL a shot for two years. Coffey also impressed at training camp and made the team. The team was no older than it had been the year before, but it was significantly more talented.

Pairing Kurri with Gretzky turned out to be one of the best moves Glen Sather ever made. Kurri finished his rookie season in Edmonton with 32 goals and 42 assists, while Gretzky eclipsed his previous year's point total with 55 goals and 109 assists to win the Art Ross trophy. The individual successes during the regular season, however, were not translating into wins on the ice. After a 4–9–5 start to the season, Sather fired head coach Bryan Watson and decided to take over the job himself. The high-flying Oilers finished the season with a 29–36–16 record, finishing in 14th place overall and again barely squeezing into the playoffs.

Their first round opponents were even more intimidating than the Philadelphia Flyers had been the year previous. The Oilers were scheduled to play *Les Glorieux* in the first round, the most revered of all teams in the NHL, the Montréal Canadiens. Although Ken Dryden was no longer their main puck stopper, the Habs still boasted a lineup full of talent and history, with Serge Savard, Steve Shutt and Guy Lafleur. The media quickly predicted another first-round exit for the Oilers, especially when they found out that Sather had given the starting goaltender's job to rookie Andy Moog, who had only played seven games during the regular season.

"I guess it's the old story of David versus Goliath," said Sather. "It's a little guy going after a big one."

Moog proved he was up to the challenge, as was the rest of the team. Edmonton came storming out of the gate in game one, building up a huge lead and settling back into a strong defensive game. When the final buzzer sounded, the Oilers had beaten the Canadiens 6–3. The press, especially those out of Montréal, thought the Oilers were just lucky. That sentiment changed when Edmonton beat the Habs 3–1 in game two. The league's newest dynamo cemented his star quality in game three when Gretzky potted his first-ever playoff hat trick to lift the Oilers to a 6–2 win over the Habs and their first-ever post-season NHL series win.

The shock and horror of the outcome could be heard echoing up and down the length of the St. Lawrence River, but the Oilers had little time to bask in their own glory. The defending Stanley

Cup champions were next, and the New York Islanders had a big bone to pick with Edmonton. Just before the series began, Gretzky had given an interview in which he declared that the team had beat Montréal because "We had to be prepared mentally and physically to beat the best team in hockey."

The New York media and players were quick to point out that it was the Islanders, the defending Stanley Cup champion, that were the best team in hockey now. Rather than complain about it, the Islanders demonstrated their point to the upstart Oilers by pounding them 8–2 in the first game, then doubling them 6–3 in game two. Gretzky pulled off another hat trick in the Oilers' game three 5–2 win, but the Islanders Ken Morrow cemented a 5–4 overtime win in game four with a shot that handcuffed Moog six minutes into the extra frame. Although the Oilers made a series of it by winning the next game 4–3, the Islanders finished them off in the sixth game of the series with a 5–2 win.

Despite Moog playing well in the playoffs, the Oilers knew heading into the draft that they needed more help in net. So Sather made Spruce Grove native Grant Fuhr, who had led the WHL in shutouts and GAA with the Victoria Cougars, their first selection in the entry draft. In what proved to be an ominous development, the

Oilers also picked London Knights defenceman Steve Smith with their sixth round selection. The remaining picks, Paul Houck, Phil Drovilland and Todd Strueby, played little if at all with the Oilers.

The 1981–82 Oilers had tasted victory and success in the post-season and were eager to dose themselves with it once again. Every single line seemed to click for the team. Gretzky elevated his play to a superhuman level many had thought him capable of, leading a high-powered Oilers offence that set a new record for total team goals in a season with 417. He was also laying waste to the NHL record books and became the fastest player to ever reach the 50-goal mark, doing so in 39 games compared to the previous record of 50 games held by both Maurice "the Rocket" Richard and Mike Bossy. He broke Phil Esposito's record for most goals in a season (76), finishing with a grand total of 92 goals and 120 assists for a record-setting total of 212 points.

As Gretzky succeeded, so too did his teammates. Mark "the Moose" Messier potted 50 goals and 38 assists, Glenn Anderson finished with 105 points and Jari Kurri with 86. Paul Coffey scored 29 goals and added 60 assists while Kevin Lowe finished the season with a plus 46. The team finished with a record of 47–21–12, first in the Smythe division and second in the league.

Everyone from the press to the fans was on their side, with some even wondering if the Oilers could finally make it to the Stanley Cup final.

The first round should have been a cakewalk. They were playing the Los Angeles Kings, who finished fourth in the Smythe that year, 48 points below the Oilers. When Edmonton jumped out to a 4–1 lead early in the first game, it was widely assumed the rest of the series would play out in a similar fashion. Yet the Kings soldiered back and won the game 10–8.

Gretzky responded in game two with an overtime goal, for a 3–2 win, and the Oilers racked up a 5–0 lead heading into the third period of game three. Again the Kings fought back and again they won, this time 6–5 in overtime. The Oilers took game four 3–2 but stumbled badly in game five. When the buzzer sounded, the Kings had beaten the Oilers 7–5 in the game and 3–2 in the best-of-five series.

"If you're going to be as cocky as this team was, you have to stay cocky," said Low. "You can't be cocky and then be overcome with self-doubts when it comes to the crunch."

The players were too young, some said, too inexperienced to handle such adversity, and to a certain extent the critics were right. The Oilers spent the entire summer listening to wave after wave of criticism of their post-season implosion, then settled their stomachs and came out fighting. With rookie Grant Fuhr now backing up Andy Moog and the Oilers firing on all cylinders, Edmonton shot through the rest of the league like a welding torch through an ice cube factory, finishing first in the Smythe again, with a record of 47–21–12 and setting a new record for total goals scored with 424. With 196 points, 71 of them goals, Gretzky was involved in almost half of all the Oilers' scoring. Messier, Anderson and Kurri each had a 100+ point season, while Paul Coffey increased his point total to 96.

With the humiliation of the previous season still fresh in their minds, Edmonton approached that year's playoffs with a determined focus that could not be disrupted. The Oilers trounced Winnipeg in the first round, swept the Flames in four games, then the Chicago Blackhawks in the Conference finals. Their appearance in the Stanley Cup finals was not so much a surprise as a requirement; now the only thing that stood between them and hockey supremacy was the defending champion, the New York Islanders.

"We want to beat them more than anything. You know why? Because they think they're the greatest thing since sliced bread," said the Islanders Clarke Gillies.

The Islanders were looking for their fourth Cup in four years, while the Oilers were looking for their first ever. Led by a stalwart, seasoned veteran corps that included Mike Bossy, Bryan Trottier, Denis Potvin, John Tonelli and goaltender Billy Smith, the Islanders took the Oilers to the school of hard knocks. Smith repelled a barrage of rubber in game one, earning a shutout and a 2–0 victory for the Islanders.

The Long Island assault continued for the next three games as New York outworked, outchecked and outscored their younger opponents. They won game two 6–3, game four 5–1 and sealed their fourth consecutive Stanley Cup win with a 4–2 win. The Islanders were too grizzled, too experienced and too determined to lose to the Oilers, but no one in the Oilers' locker room seemed to understand that. The Islanders had shut down Wayne Gretzky, who had managed only four assists during the final series. All the Oilers could see was that they had had their chance, and they had come up short.

The 1983–84 entry draft proved to be the last of its kind for Edmonton, but no one at the time understood that. The Oilers took punishing defenceman Jeff Beukeboom with their 19th pick in the first round, a few less noteworthy forwards with their next two picks, then again looked across the Atlantic and plucked pesky, talented left winger Esa Tikkanen from HIFK Helsinki. It would not be until the 1990s that the Oilers would successfully draft a player who would excel with the team later on.

Over the summer, the team again began to retool and retrench. The coming season was immaterial. Winning the Smythe division no longer mattered. Only the Stanley Cup would satisfy the Oilers' desires.

Chapter Three

The Glory Years

If the 1982–83 Oilers had been a determined bunch, then the 1983–84 Oilers were as committed a group of hockey players as had ever taken the ice.

Having digested the ins and outs, the what ifs and should haves of their Stanley Cup final sweep at the hands of the New York Islanders, the Oilers knew they had the talent to get to the end of hockey's second season. Having seen the Islanders in their dressing room pressing ice packs against bruised bones and muscles and having cuts sewn shut, the Oilers now knew it would take more than just pure talent to become the NHL champs. It would take both heart and soul.

The season was barely a month old when Sather began making the necessary moves that would bring that extra element of grit and tenacity to the Oilers lineup. In November, Sather traded Tom Roulston to Pittsburgh for banger Kevin McClelland, a right winger with relatively soft hands for his size. McClelland complemented Sather's previous additions of red-haired defenceman Randy Gregg and Flyers centre Ken Linesman. As the season progressed, Sather shipped burnout Don Murdoch to Minnesota for defenceman Don Jackson, then signed 30-year-old Czech left winger Jaroslav Pouzar to the team. In one final move, Sather traded Laurie Boschman to Winnipeg to acquire Swedish forward Willy Lindstrom, already 32 years old.

What followed was creation of a style of play known as "firewagon hockey," or as the Oilers put it, "Five up" hockey. The Oilers' objective in any game was simply to outscore their opponents, and every member of the team had a role to play. While Gretzky, Kurri, Messier and Anderson fronted the bulk of the offence, the remainder of the team was expected to maintain the fiery, fast-paced brand of hockey that effectively overwhelmed an opponent's defence. The Oilers' style of hockey came with one price: goaltender Grant Fuhr, who was now taking over from Moog as the Oilers' starting netminder, was more often than not left to his own devices when other teams managed to turn the play the other way. It was not uncommon for Fuhr to stop upwards of 30 shots per game. Although his GAA during his time with the Oilers seldom dipped below the 3.00 mark, it didn't need to because Edmonton was scoring four, five or six goals per game. Fuhr only needed to make the big stops, which gave the rest of the team the confidence of knowing that he had their back when they were up crashing the other team's net. It was a role Fuhr relished and excelled at.

Gretzky, of course, led the Oilers in scoring, reaching the 200-point plateau for the second time in his career by potting 87 goals and 118 assists. He also added a 51-game point-scoring streak, the longest in history. Jari Kurri scored 52 goals, while Glenn Anderson managed 54 of his own. Despite these performances, it was defenceman Paul Coffey who finished second in both team and league scoring with 40 goals and 86 assists.

The team as a whole finished with a record of 57–18–5, 37 points ahead of the Smythe's second-place Flames and also good enough for first in the league. The Oilers again broke their own record for goals in season, lighting the red lamp a total of 446 times.

They again sailed through the first three rounds of the playoffs like a team possessed. They outscored the Winnipeg Jets in total 18–7 over three games to win the first series but slowed down a bit against the Flames in the Smythe final, needing seven games to dispatch their hated Alberta rivals. The team ramped up their play in the Conference finals and swept the Minnesota

North Stars in four straight games, earning a nine-game rest before they took on the New York Islanders for the Stanley Cup.

"When it happens, I'd like to feel like the team that beat us earned their victory like we've earned ours," said Islanders' defenceman Denis Potvin.

History, however, was not in the Oilers' favour. They had not beaten the Islanders, neither in the regular season nor in playoffs, in 10 games. New York was looking to tie the Montréal Canadiens as one of the only teams to win five Stanley Cups in a row. The Islanders trotted out their same assembly of seasoned, high-scoring pros while the Oilers countered with their slightly augmented lineup, including Grant Fuhr in goal.

Fuhr was sensational in game one, stopping 38 shots on goal, matching Billy Smith save for save. In the end, it was one of the new Oilers, Kevin McClelland, who scored the game's only goal to give the Oilers a 1–0 win and a one-game lead in the Stanley Cup final series. The Islanders stormed back in game two, starting Rolland Melanson in net instead of Billy Smith, and trumped Edmonton 6–1.

Paul Coffey took matters into his own hands in game three, scoring two goals 17 seconds apart during a 4-on-4 situation. Both goals seemed like mere insurance markers when the final buzzer sounded and the Oilers posted a 7–2 win over the

Islanders. Game four, though won by a similar score, came at a higher price because Grant Fuhr left the game with a bruised shoulder.

The Oilers were now up three games to one in the series and one win away from hockey's penultimate prize.

"Belief. That's the biggest barrier we had to overcome. I mean, it's tough for a team to believe they can beat the four-time Stanley Cup champions. But now we believe," said Paul Coffey.

Although Fuhr's injury was cause for concern, Andy Moog's play was not. The BC native was brilliant off the bench, holding the Islanders to only two goals. The Oilers responded with five of their own, and before the buzzer even sounded they were jumping into one another's arms, dog-piling on Moog and celebrating a dream that had been several years in the making. The upstart, firewagon team, who could score seemingly at will, had finally found the extra push necessary to propel them to supremacy. In the end, it was not Gretzky with his 13 goals and 22 assists who was named the playoff MVP, but Mark Messier, who scored eight goals and added 18 assists. Messier had played with grit and ferocity, something the Oilers had lacked the last time around.

The core of the team had little in the way of time off. That summer, the second inaugural Canada Cup was being held, pitting Canada's best hockey players against the professional players from Europe. Gretzky, Fuhr, Coffey, Messier, Anderson, Lowe, Gregg and Huddy were all named to the team. Team Canada stumbled slightly in the round robin, finishing with a 2–2–1 record and playing the dreaded Red Machine of the USSR in the semifinal. The game was tied 2–2 going into the final minutes of the third period when Paul Coffey successfully intercepted a pass during a Soviet two-on-one and drove the play back up ice into the Soviet zone. Coffey then fired a shot on goal that Mike Bossy tipped home to win the game and propel the Canadians to the final, where they beat Sweden in two straight to win the Canada Cup.

The Oilers team that took to the ice in 1984–85 needed little in the way of change, but Sather decided to tweak the lineup a little bit. He traded Ken Linseman to the Boston Bruins for forward Mike Krushelnyski and acquired Mark Napier from Minnesota. The rest of the team, however, remained essentially intact and picked up in the regular season where they had left off the previous spring. Gretzky recorded his second-straight 200-point season, finishing the regular year with 73 goals and 135 assists. Kurri came into his own, scoring 71 times while newcomer Mike Krushelnyski added 43 goals, followed by Anderson with 42 goals. Fuhr again played the most of the Oilers goaltenders, recording 26 wins and a 3.87 GAA in 46 games between the pipes.

A return to the Stanley Cup finals seemed inevitable for Edmonton, who finished with 49 wins, second only in the league to Philadelphia. The Oilers dispatched the Kings in three straight games in the first round of the playoffs, with two games going to overtime. The Oilers continued their "stop hitting yourself" post-season record with Winnipeg, sweeping the Jets in four straight games before lighting up the Blackhawks Murray Bannerman for 44 goals in a six-game series that featured 11–2 and 10–5 wins by the Oilers.

Their opponents in the Stanley Cup final, however, were not their enemies of years past. The Islanders were no longer in the playoffs, replaced instead by the Philadelphia Flyers. Led by Swedish goaltending sensation Pelle Lindbergh, the Flyers actually caught the Oilers napping in game one of the series, winning the opener 4–1. It was the last time the Flyers would be so lucky.

"The slow start had me awfully concerned," said Sather. "I chewed my nails to the quick. We got ourselves out of an enormous hole. It seemed like they'd brought the pucks from Philly."

Lindbergh had started a practice that has since become commonplace but at the time was viewed with some skepticism. The Flyers goalie found that he became dehydrated quickly during a game and consequently started keeping a water bottle on top of his net. The Oilers couldn't seem to accept why this would be a good idea and, as the series progressed, decided to make an issue of it in the media and with the league. Sather commented that Lindbergh shouldn't be allowed to set up a "lunch buffet in his net." Glenn Anderson asked the media rhetorically, "What is he going to want up there next, a bucket of fried chicken?"

The league agreed with the Oilers and banned Lindbergh from using the bottle. His play consequently began to suffer as the Oilers picked the Flyers apart with their speed, passing and shooting. Edmonton won the next four games by scores of 3–1, 4–3, 5–3 and 8–3. By game four, Lindbergh was so tired and dehydrated that backup goalie Bob Froese actually tended the pipes for the Flyers.

"We all get our names on the Stanley Cup. That's all that matters," said Gretzky. "We've got to be rated as good as any team that ever won two in a row. All I know is that 15 years from now, I'm going to say 'Gawd, I played on a great hockey team.'"

It was the Oilers' second Cup in two years, but the magic of the moment was not lost on anyone. Their performance in the 1985 playoffs was one

of sheer dominance. Gretzky was named the winner of the Conn Smythe trophy, setting a playoff
scoring record with 17 goals and 30 assists. Kurri
set the playoff record for goals with 19, including
four hat tricks, while Paul Coffey set a record for
playoff scoring for a defenceman, with 12 goals
and 25 assists.

The hardware kept coming for the Oilers.
Gretzky again won the Art Ross and Hart
Trophies, but he was not alone on the awards
podium. After finishing second to Rod Langway
the year previous, Paul Coffey was awarded the
Norris Trophy as the best defenceman in the
league, and Kurri took home the Lady Byng for
most gentlemanly player.

Edmonton had been so dominant in 1984–85
that there was no reason to think they wouldn't
three-peat. Hell, the media thought, this Oilers
team stood every chance of matching the
Montréal Canadiens for five straight Cup wins,
maybe even exceeding it.

The team that showed up for the 1985–86
season was again essentially the same team but
with a few exceptions. Sather made two key
additions during the season, adding Pittsburgh
defenceman and known pugilist Marty McSorley to the blueline. He also extended an olive
branch to a character player who everyone
thought was finished in the league. The previous

year, Bruins centre Craig MacTavish had been jailed on a charge of vehicular manslaughter for killing a woman in a drunk driving accident. When he was released from jail, Sather signed him to a contract. Besides his checkered past, "Mac-T" stood out in the league for another reason: he would become the last player in the NHL to play without a helmet.

The coaching staff changed as well. Sather made John Muckler "co-coach," and assistant Ted Green, upset there might be little chance for advancement with Muckler now dubbed the heir apparent, left the team to open his own skate-sharpening business. Bob McCammon was hired in his place.

The changes, however, served only to make the Oilers better. In 1985–86, the Oilers posted one of the greatest records in NHL history, finishing the year with a 56–17–7 record to tie their previous high of 119 points and secure first place in the league. Gretzky was, again, Gretzky, finishing the season with 215 points. Kurri banged home 68 goals, Anderson scored 54 times, and Coffey stepped up his play to score 48 goals, breaking Bobby Orr's record for most goals by a defenceman. Coffey also finished second in team scoring again, with 138 points.

The Oilers blew by the Canucks in the first round of the playoffs, winning three straight games to face the Calgary Flames in the second round for the Smythe division championship. The Flames were now led by former Islanders mainstay John Tonelli and featured Mike Vernon, a short sparkplug of a goaltender, between the pipes. The Battle of Alberta was already known as one of the greatest rivalries in all of sport, but in this year's playoffs, the provincial war had some unexpected casualties.

Calgary took the Oilers by surprise in game one of the second-round series, rolling to a 4–1 win. The Oilers bounced back, squeaking out a 6–5 win in overtime to tie the series at one, but then surrendered a 3–2 loss in game three to give the Flames a 2–1 lead in the series. Edmonton stormed back in game four, winning it 7–4, but Calgary took a death grip on the series with a 4–1 win in game five. On the verge of elimination for the first time in two years, the Oilers came out and played hard in game six, winning 5–2 and setting the stage for the most dramatic of all hockey games, a winner-take-all game seven.

The game did not start well for the Oilers. Calgary opened the scoring twice, jumping out to a 2–0 lead. Slowly, the Oilers fought back. Glenn Anderson scored first, halving the Flames' lead before Mark Messier tied the game at two. With a little under six minutes left, barring some sort of defensive lapse, it looked as if game seven was heading to a sudden-death overtime finish.

The day was Steve Smith's 23rd birthday. The young defenceman, drafted the same year as Grant Fuhr, had seen some action the previous year in two games before playing 55 games in the 1985–86 campaign. With 5:18 left in the third period of game seven, Smith took the puck behind the Oilers net, stopped, then threw a breakout pass from behind the goal up the middle.

Oilers fans watched in horror as the unthinkable happened. The puck scarcely moved when it banked off of Grant Fuhr's skate and trickled into the Edmonton goal. Everyone on the ice, in the crowd, and watching the game on TV was stunned as Smith collapsed to his knees on the ice. As the last Flame to touch the puck, Perry Berezan was credited with the goal, which turned out to be the winner. Although the Oilers threw everything they had at the Flames, Calgary held on for the win. When the final buzzer sounded, the Flames rejoiced while the Oilers collectively hung their heads.

"I've got to keep on living. I don't know if I'll ever live this down, but I have to keep on living. The sun will come up tomorrow," said Smith. "The players have stuck by me. But this is just a time I have to spend by myself right now. It was a human error. I'll have to live by it."

For the first time in three years, the Oilers spent the bulk of their post-season either at home or on a golf course. The fans in Edmonton had at first roared for Smith's head on a platter, but the din eventually died down to a barely discernible mumbling. That discontent was overshadowed weeks later by a series of stunning revelations that left many wondering exactly what kind of players these Oilers were.

On May 12, *Sports Illustrated*, a weekly sports magazine with more of a preference for football and baseball than for hockey, published a feature story in which the magazine alleged that five members of the Edmonton Oilers had substance abuse problems. Although the article never named which of the five Oilers were rumoured to abuse drugs, it implied that the drugs of choice were marijuana and cocaine. The Oilers dismissed the story as fundamentally untrue. Yet the Oilers were not known for their schoolboy behaviour in what was now called "The City of Champions." Mark Messier had crashed his Porsche earlier in the season, and Dave Hunter had been in and out of jail for driving under the influence three times during the last two years.

The Oilers' problems didn't just stop with the members of the team. On June 1, 1985, over 1000 employees of Gainers, a meatpacking company owned by Peter Pocklington, walked off the job. Pocklington refused to concede to the union, and he used strikebreakers and eventually the police to get scab workers through the picket line. The strike was not only a nuisance for Pocklington; it was expensive.

The Oilers didn't just lose the Stanley Cup; they also started missing out on some of the individual hardware they had grown accustomed to winning at the end of every season. Gretzky again won the Hart Trophy but was denied the Pearson Award by a young, exceptionally talented Frenchman with an attitude problem. Mario Lemieux, whose hands were as soft as Gretzky's, was rumoured to be Gretzky's successor as the NHL's superstar player. He had Gretzky's hands and vision, plus an extra few inches to match his tremendous size.

Despite Lemieux's growing supremacy, Pocklington sat down with Gretzky and his agent Mike Barnett and hammered out a new, four-year deal for Gretzky, with an option for a fifth year. The agreement did not contain a no-trade clause, which might be expected of a team trying to hang on to its greatest asset, but it did give Gretzky the right to retire any time he chose.

In addition, the face of the Edmonton Oilers slowly started to shift. Sather traded Dave Semenko, Gretzky's long-time enforcer and protector, to Hartford for a third-round draft pick. Sather also shipped Donnie Jackson and Mike Golden to the New York Rangers for the rights to forward Reijo Ruotsalainen, then sent Lee Fogolin and Mark Napier to Buffalo for Norm Lacombe and Wayne Van Dorp. In one last move, Sather gave up a draft pick to Minnesota for forward Kent Nilsson.

As the Gainers strike continued and the new season dawned, the hockey world was wondering how the Oilers would react to their unexpected elimination from the post-season.

Chapter Four

The Beginning of the End

The Calgary Flames were turning into the Edmonton Oilers' foil in the NHL.

The Flames went to the Stanley Cup finals after barely bouncing the Oilers from the post-season the previous year. During the championship series Calgary ran into a young, twitchy Québec goaltender named Patrick Roy, who was now the main puckstopper for the Montréal Canadiens. The Habs unceremoniously dumped the Flames in five games, winning the Stanley Cup.

But as the 1986–87 season progressed, the Oilers couldn't shake the Flames. The humiliation of the playoff defeat the previous season had not been forgotten, and yet the Flames still owned the Oilers during the regular season, winning the battle of Alberta four times, losing once and tying Edmonton once.

Those four losses, however, were only a handful the Oilers suffered all season long. Although their performance was not as dramatic as their 1985–86 season, the Oilers managed 50 wins in 1986–87, finishing the year with 106 points, good enough again for first overall in the league. Gretzky again led the Oilers in scoring with 62 goals and 121 assists, followed by Jari Kurri's 54 goals and 54 assists. Despite their record the 1986–87 Oilers were not the offensive juggernauts of years past. Only Gretzky and Kurri scored more than 50 goals—Anderson slipped to 35, Coffey to 16 and Krushelnyski to 15. Esa Tikkanen, who had made his debut with the Oilers during their 1985 Stanley Cup final against the Flyers, was the pleasant surprise of the season, scoring 34 goals and adding 44 assists.

"This season really dragged on," said Messier. "This year, more than any other, seemed to go on forever. We didn't care as much about finishing first and accomplishing a lot of things that used to be important to us. The playoffs are where it's at. We never knew it as much as we knew it this year."

Grant Fuhr and Andy Moog were still splitting most of the games in Edmonton, but Fuhr was favoured as the Oilers' playoff starter, a fact that began to grate on Moog. Nonetheless, the Oilers finished the season in first place and started their annual tear through the first round of the play-offs. They dispatched the Kings in five games, setting an NHL record for most goals in a playoff game with a 13–3 win. Again they pummeled the Winnipeg Jets, sweeping them in four games before defeating the Detroit Red Wings in five games in the Conference final. The Oilers' opponents in the Stanley Cup final ended up being the Philadelphia Flyers.

These Flyers were not the Flyers of 1985. Pelle Lindbergh was dead, killed in a drunk driving crash when he piled his sports car into a guardrail. In his place stood Ron Hextall, a goaltender with a temper and a penchant for using his goal stick to keep his crease clear. Mike Keenan was still behind the bench, an authoritarian hockey genius who demanded nothing less than from his players than their full effort.

The Oilers were ready for the Flyers. Before play shifted to Philadelphia, the Oilers had gained a 2–0 lead in the series. The Flyers squeaked out a 5–3 win on home ice in game three but dropped game four 4–1. Although the Oilers took a 3–1 lead home to Northlands Coliseum, the Flyers refused to cave in and posted 4–3 and 3–2 wins to tie the series at three games apiece. In the game seven that ensued, there were no mistakes. Sather outthought Keenan, and Fuhr outplayed Hextall as the Oilers won the game 3–1. The Oilers had now won their third Stanley Cup in four years, effectively banishing the demons of 1986 to the attic of history.

"This is the greatest," said Kevin Lowe. "We won the Stanley Cup in the seventh game. You can't compare the other two to this one. We'll remember this one the most."

No one on the ice that night knew that it was the last time they would see this core group of players celebrate a Stanley Cup championship.

The Canada Cup was on again that summer, and Edmonton was well represented. Glenn Anderson, Paul Coffey, Wayne Gretzky and Mark Messier all played, while Grant Fuhr started every game for Team Canada. Oilers co-coach John Muckler served as Mike Keenan's assistant, and they guided the squad to a 6–1–2 record in the tournament. Inevitably, the Canadians faced off against the Red Machine of the USSR in the best of three final. After trading 6–5 wins in the first two games, the championship came down to the third game of the series. With only seconds left on the clock, linemates Wayne Gretzky and Mario Lemieux broke out of the Canadian zone on the Russian defenders. Gretzky fed a pass to Lemieux, who waited a second before roofing the puck into the top corner of the Russian goal.

The celebration was short-lived. As soon as Team Canada disbanded, several Oilers began to make their discontent with the team known.

Mark Messier and Paul Coffey refused to report to training camp in an effort to negotiate new contracts. Both were suspended. Andy Moog, who had grown increasingly unhappy sharing his ice time with Grant Fuhr the last three years, also decided to hold out and demanded a trade. When the trade was slow in coming, Moog signed up with Team Canada for the 1988 Olympics in Calgary, along with Randy Gregg. Glenn Anderson returned to the fold after a brief holdout, but Kent Nilsson and Reijo Ruotsalainen decided to return to Europe.

In the end, Mark Messier was awarded a new six-year deal, but Coffey was not willing to return. Pocklington spoke to the media and openly questioned the defenceman's courage. Once he got wind of that, Coffey declared that there was no way he could play for the Oilers again. On November 24, Sather dealt Coffey to the Pittsburgh Penguins along with Dave Hunter and Wayne Van Dorp in exchange for Craig Simpson, Chris Joseph, Moe Mantha and Davey Hannan.

"You always wonder when you trade a guy like Paul whether or not you made the right trade," said Sather. "It doesn't matter who you get back, you can't replace Coffey. Paul is just coming into the best years of his career, but his attitude changed to the point where he couldn't reconcile the situation here."

After a strong but medal-less performance in Calgary, the Oilers traded Moog to the Boston Bruins, where he was guaranteed more playing time. In exchange, the Oilers received goaltender Bill Ranford and forward Geoff Courtnall.

The 1987–88 Oilers were not the dominant force of years past. Edmonton finished second in the Smythe division and third overall, behind Calgary and Montréal. Gretzky was sidelined by a knee injury and played only 64 games but still led the Oilers in scoring with 40 goals and 109 assists. Craig Simpson fit into the lineup nicely, scoring 43 in his first year as an Oiler, while Kurri also potted 43. Grant Fuhr played a league-record 75 games, winning 40 games and posting a 3.43 goals against average.

By this point, no one knew what to expect from the Oilers in the upcoming playoffs. The Winnipeg Jets actually gave the Oilers a bit of a challenge, winning one game on home ice. But Craig Simpson scored two game-winning goals in the first two games. The Oilers came back from a 3–0 deficit to win game four by 5–3 before icing Winnipeg again with a 6–2 win in game five.

The Oilers drew the Flames for the Smythe division championships and headed into the series as the underdogs, with the Flames having finished six points ahead of them in the regular season standings. The Oilers showed that regular season success was not an indicator of post-season victory. After winning the first game 3–1, Gretzky scored the overtime winner while the Oilers were shorthanded in game two to give the Oilers a 5–4 win. The Oilers went on to win game three 4–2 and game four 6–4, knocking the Flames out of the playoffs.

The Detroit Red Wings yielded in five games in the Conference final, setting the stage for a dramatic Stanley Cup championship. Andy Moog's Bruins had won the Wales Conference and the former Oilers netminder would now battle his former teammates for hockey's ultimate prize. Rather than try to pound the Bruins into submission with their offensive brand of hockey, the Oilers tightened up defensively, limiting the Bruins to only 26 shots in the first two games, both of which the Oilers won.

After winning game three by a score of 6–3, Edmonton went into Boston ready to take the series. With the fourth game tied 3–3 in the second period, the lights at the aging Boston Gardens suddenly went out and did not come back on. Game officials reluctantly rescheduled the game, but instead of playing the game in Boston, both teams headed back to Edmonton for the second game four. In front of their hometown crowd, the Oilers racked up a 6–3 win to secure their fourth Stanley Cup in five years. Gretzky was again named the MVP of the playoffs. After the win, the Oilers started a tradition that has been repeated in every Stanley Cup final since—they all collapsed around the Cup for a team photo.

"It was done for everybody, the players and the people who have been behind this team for so long. Nobody has ever done something like this before. It was a great idea," said Sather.

There was little time for Wayne Gretzky to savour his fourth Stanley Cup victory. The Oilers all-star player had his mind set on a new focus that had nothing to do with hockey but had everything to do with the future of his team. He was getting married.

Gretzky had dated a woman in Edmonton named Vicki Moss for several years before breaking off the relationship. Shortly afterwards, he met Janet Jones at a Los Angeles Lakers game. Jones was a beautiful actress whose most significant role in movies had been in the films *A Chorus Line* and *American Anthem*. She'd also been a Playboy girl. The courtship had been fast and furious before Gretzky popped the question; Jones said yes.

The Gretzky-Jones marriage took place in Edmonton, at St. Joseph's Basilica. It was the city's equivalent of a royal wedding, with dignitaries and team members all invited to the festivities. Several members of the team served as the Great One's groomsmen at the July 16 wedding, and comedian Alan Thicke hosted the reception. After the ceremony was over, the newly married couple waved to the crowds who had gathered outside the Basilica, hoping to catch a glimpse of Gretzky and his new bride.

Although Gretzky was smiling, he must have been wracked by a terrible anxiety during the ceremony, because his days in Edmonton were numbered. Only a day after the Oilers won their fourth Stanley Cup, Pocklington approached Gretzky and told him that he was going to try to trade him.

Pocklington was in dire need of cash, and Gretzky was by far his most valuable asset. The ordeal with Gainers was costing Puck approximately $1 million per day, and he had already been forced to put the company up as collateral for a $55 million loan from the Alberta Treasury Branch.

"I'd like to say I knew it was coming, but I must admit I thought Wayne Gretzky would never leave Edmonton. It's very hard for me to believe," said Canadian hockey iconoclast Don Cherry.

Gretzky, meanwhile, was beginning to fade ever so slightly as the game's dominant superstar. He had lost the scoring title the previous season to Mario Lemieux, scoring only 40 goals. He had missed several games because of a knee injury, and that same injury brought into question his durability. He was by no means old—not yet even 30—but his goal totals had dropped in each of the previous three seasons. Like it or not, Gretzky was on his way down and also on the way out of Edmonton.

Sather at first tried to trade Wayne to the Rangers but couldn't come up with a satisfactory deal. And then, five days before Wayne's wedding, Los Angeles Kings owner Bruce McNall called Gretzky in an effort to win him over to his side and to allow himself to be traded to the Kings. Knowing there was nothing he could do to prolong his career in Edmonton, Gretzky agreed, but he insisted on telling the press and the public that it had been his idea, in order to spare Pocklington and the rest of the team the backlash that would follow from the team's fans and boosters.

August 9 in Edmonton is now referred to as Black Sunday, for it was on that day Pocklington convened a press conference. The media assembled to find Gretzky, Pocklington and McNall seated at a table at the front of the room. In a slow, haunting tone, Pocklington announced that the Oilers had traded Wayne Gretzky, one of their original players since they had made the leap from the WHA. The Oilers' all-time leading goal and point scorer and team captain was going to the Los Angeles Kings. Pocklington yielded the microphone to Gretzky who began to speak. As he tried to find the words, he eventually started to cry, then laughed and said he had "promised Mess I wouldn't do this." Gretzky stuck to the script, insisting it had been his idea to be traded and that the trade to L.A. suited his purposes, especially given his recent marriage to a Hollywood actress. He also revealed at the press conference that Janet, his new wife, was pregnant.

Along with Gretzky, the Oilers shipped enforcer Marty McSorley as well as forward Mike Krushelnyski to the Kings. In exchange for the three players, Pocklington personally got a $15 million cash infusion. The team received forward Jimmy Carter, recently drafted forward Martin Gelinas, along with the Los Angeles Kings first round draft selection in 1989, 1991 and 1993. Gretzky himself received $5 million for going along with the deal.

The trade outraged the entire city of Edmonton. Radio call-in shows were crammed with angry fans who took turns vilifying Peter Pocklington, Wayne Gretzky and even Janet Jones, for their role in taking the Great One away from Edmonton. Through it all, Pocklington maintained that it was all Gretzky's idea. In an interview after the trade was complete, Pocklington told the *Edmonton Journal* that Gretzky had "an ego the size of Manhattan." He also insinuated that Wayne had been acting when he'd started crying during the press conference.

"He's a great actor," Pocklington went on to say.

No one who saw the video footage of the press conference agreed with Puck. To everyone else besides him, the tears appeared to be genuine.

The changes over the summer had an effect on the team, and it began to slowly unravel. With Coffey and Moog gone, and now Gretzky as well, the Oilers needed to acquire new young talent to start taking their places. Yet the Oilers had not drafted well over the last few years, ever since they had taken Esa Tikkanen. The first round selections of Selmar Odelien, Scott Metcalfe, Kim Issell, Peter Soberlack and Francois Leroux never made it to the big leagues. There were some notable exceptions—forward Kelly Buchburger was picked 188th overall in the 1985 draft, and he saw some ice time in the playoffs. In 1987 the Oilers drafted Geoff Smith 63rd overall and took Shaun Van Allen with their 105th selection.

So the Oilers team that took to the ice for the 1988–89 season didn't look that much different from the team that had won the Stanley Cup four months earlier, but it was different. Gretzky's absence was glaring to every single fan who had watched him play. Jimmy Carson turned out to be a potent offensive talent, scoring 49 goals and 51 assists, while Kurri proved that he was still an offensive force to be reckoned with, leading the team with 44 goals and 58 assists for total scoring. Mark Messier, Esa Tikkanen and Craig Simpson all chipped in 30 or more goals, and the Oilers finished their first season without the Great One with a respectable 38–34–8 record, good enough for third place in the Smythe division. As luck would have it, the Oilers' third place finish meant that they would take on the Los Angeles Kings in the first round of the playoffs.

Gretzky did well with the Kings, leading the team that had been rebranded with new jerseys to a respectable finish in the 1988–89 season. He again finished behind Mario Lemieux in the scoring race but won the Hart Trophy as the league's most valuable player. Gretzky had made hockey a popular sport in Los Angeles, a city where it never snows. The team's games sold out the entire year at home, and the best seats in the house were often lined with Hollywood movie stars who had come to see what this new Canadian hockey player was all about.

The Oilers came to the series ready to show Gretzky that they didn't need him to succeed in the NHL post-season, and for a while it looked as though they could do just that. They won the first game of the series 4–3, then dropped the second to the Kings by a score of 5–2. Edmonton blanked Los Angeles in game three by a score of 4–0, then squeaked out a 4–3 win in game four to take a 3–1 lead in the series. It did seem as if the Oilers really didn't need Gretzky. Few teams in the history of the NHL had come back from a 3–1 deficit in any round of the playoffs, let alone the first.

The Kings, however, weren't ready to give up. Led by their newest acquisition Wayne Gretzky, and with Marty McSorley patrolling the ice and daring any of his former teammates to lay a hand on the Great One, the Kings won game five of the series 4–2 to draw within one game of Edmonton. The Oilers weren't worried yet, but the mild surprise of losing game five gave way to a renewed sense of panic when the Kings also won game six, posting a 4–1 score. Again the Oilers faced a game seven opponent, but this single series meant more than any series had before. The Oilers were trying to show Wayne Gretzky that they didn't need him anymore, that their team was still strong, still a contender without him in their lineup.

Apparently, the Oilers were wrong. Despite their best efforts, the Kings finished off the Oilers with a 6–3 win on home ice. It was the first playoff series the Oilers had lost since dropping the 1986 Smythe division final to the Flames.

"I feel deeply sorry for the Edmonton players, especially Mark and Kevin," Gretzky said after the game. "I wanted to talk to them but couldn't. No one takes losing as hard as those two guys. We just beat the best playoff team in the league."

The Kings never got past the Calgary Flames, who went on to the Stanley Cup finals to take on the Canadiens for the Stanley Cup final. It was a repeat of the 1986 series, though this time Patrick Roy did not play up to his usual sensational standard. The Flames beat the Habs in six games, taking home their first Stanley Cup in franchise history.

As the Oilers dispersed at the end of the season, everyone had a sense that something wasn't quite right. There was a feeling that the team would eventually look quite different than it had this year. And this year they'd been without their greatest player.

It started only months later. In June 1989, goaltender Grant Fuhr filed his retirement papers.

Chapter Five

One Last Gasp

Fuhr's retirement was brief. He returned to the Oilers for training camp but just as quickly bowed back out after having an appendectomy on September 14. He eventually recovered from his appendectomy but injured his left shoulder in a game on December 16, again handing the starting job back to Bill Ranford. The resulting reconstructive surgery knocked Fuhr out of the lineup until March. Ten days later, he injured the shoulder again. Ranford, acquired from the Boston Bruins in the Andy Moog trade, took over the starting position for the beginning of the season. Glen Sather announced he would cede the coaching duties to John Muckler and work full time as the team's general manager.

"It's an easy transition. I've been with John Muckler for a long time, and it seems I've been with Teddy Green all my life. It's not like I'm passing on this job to somebody I don't know or trust," Sather said.

Four games into the season, Jimmy Carson, one of the players the Oilers had acquired from the Kings in exchange for Gretzky, announced that he would rather retire than play another year for the Oilers. Sather quickly traded him to the Detroit Red Wings along with Kevin McClelland. In exchange, the Oilers received Joe Murphy, Jeff Sharples, Adam Graves and Petr Klima, who seemed to fit into the lineup well.

The season had barely started when Wayne Gretzky returned to Northlands Coliseum as a member of the Los Angeles Kings. Gretzky had already played in Edmonton a few times, but this game was more meaningful than any of the others to date. When the Kings landed in Edmonton on October 15, Gretzky was tied with Gordie Howe for the most points ever scored by any NHL player in the history of the game with 1850. One more point would make Gretzky the league's all-time leading scorer.

It seemed fitting then that the first chance Gretzky had to break the record was against his old team in Edmonton. Although some of the players had changed, Kevin Lowe, Mark Messier and Glen Sather were still wearing the Oilers copper and blue. After two-and-a-half periods of play, the Oilers were leading the Kings. It looked as if Gretzky's record-setting attempt would have to wait for another day.

Then, with minutes remaining in the period, Gretzky grabbed a rebound and slipped it past a sprawling Bill Ranford, scoring the 1851st point of his career.

Northlands Coliseum was jammed to the rafters, and every person in attendance erupted with joy, overlooking the fact that Gretzky had just denied their Oilers a victory. The game stopped, the Oilers unrolled a red carpet, and Gretzky took centre ice to receive a succession of gifts from the Kings, the league and the Oilers. When the party broke up and the game resumed, Gretzky picked up his stick and scored the winning goal for the Los Angeles Kings.

Whereas October's game between the Kings and Oilers had been one big love-in in which the city of Edmonton welcomed home the son who had left so unexpectedly, a February 28 game between both teams turned decidedly ugly. The Los Angeles game became one of the most violent in the history of the NHL—both teams combined for 85 penalties, totaling a new league record of 365 minutes. Edmonton was responsible for 44 of the penalties: 26 were minor penalties, seven were majors, six were 10-minute misconducts, four were game misconducts and one was a match penalty. Whatever good humour had existed between the two teams seemed to evaporate in the course of a single night.

With Gretzky now gone, Mark Messier stepped into the role as leader of the Edmonton Oilers. Besides being the team captain, Messier led the Oilers in scoring in 1989–90 with 45 goals and 84 assists, which was also good enough for second place in league scoring, behind Mario Lemieux. He didn't just play big; he talked big.

As Edmonton struggled through November with one of its worst-ever records, Messier proclaimed to the press, "We're going to win the Stanley Cup this year."

Tikkanen, Kurri and Anderson all eclipsed the 30-goal mark, while newcomers Petr Klima, Adam Graves and Joe Murphy managed 25, 9 and 7 goals respectively. Ranford, taking over from the injured Fuhr, proved he was more than capable of handling the starting job, winning 24 of 56 games while posting a 3.19 GAA and a 0.887 save percentage.

The team again managed to win 38 games, good enough for second place in the Smythe division behind the Calgary Flames. Even though the Oilers were scheduled to play the Winnipeg Jets in the first round, a team the Oilers had owned in the first season, no one was predicting the Oilers would do much in the year's playoffs.

And for a time it didn't seem as though the Oilers would make it past the first round. Edmonton dropped the first game to Winnipeg by a score of 7–5, then salvaged a 3–2 win in game two. Winnipeg, however, jumped forward to grab a 3–1 stranglehold in the series with a 2–1 win in game three and a 4–3 win in game four. Rather than fold, the Oilers kept banging away at the Jets, squeaking out 4–3 wins in games five and six to tie the series at three games apiece. Game seven was something of a non-event as the Oilers rolled to a 4–1 victory that propelled them into the second round of the playoffs.

The second round series against Gretzky and the Los Angeles Kings had nothing to do with sentiment or friendly ties. It had everything to do with winning. Eager to avenge their first-round defeat at the Kings' hands the previous season, the Oilers unleashed a fury of offence on Los Angeles, winning four straight games by scores of 7–0, 6–1, 5–4 and 6–5. Gretzky was a non-factor in the series, but Bill Ranford, who had assumed the starting role in the playoffs, was proving he could play in the clutch. The tall, lanky Canadian was the last of a dying breed, a stand-up goaltender who had quick feet and an even faster glove hand.

"They could pretty much be unstoppable," Gretzky said after the final game. "Messier keeps getting stronger and stronger, and if Ranford continues to be as tough as he was in this series...A lot of people forget they won the Cup two years ago."

Edmonton next hosted Chicago in the Campbell Conference finals, and here, the media thought, was where Edmonton would finally come unglued. The Oilers silenced their critics with a 5–2 win in the first game, then gave them more fuel with disappointing 4–3 and 5–1 losses in games two and three. But two games were all Chicago could manage. The Oilers won the next three games in a row by scores of 4–2, 4–3 and 8–4. They had done something that no one in the league thought they had talent to do anymore. The Edmonton Oilers had made it to the Stanley Cup finals.

Their opponent's face was as familiar as Gretzky's, if not more so. Boston still had Andy Moog tending the pipes, along with a potent offence led by hard-hitting winger Cam Neely. No one was ready to pick a winner in the series, and both teams went into game one with an equal mixture of nerves and determination. At the end of regulation, the game was tied at two. The first overtime period resulted in no winner. The second overtime period ended with the teams still tied at two. It was not until 55:13 of the third overtime period, almost one more full game after the original game had started, that Petr Klima, who hadn't yet played a shift in overtime, pocketed the winning goal for the Oilers to give them a 1–0 series lead.

"When I got the shot, I didn't just shoot, I shot for the five-hole between Andy Moog's legs. At 1:30 in the morning, you have to make a good shot," said Klima.

The second game was less of an ordeal than the first had been as the Oilers rolled to an easy 7–2 win. The Bruins pushed the Oilers hard in game three and etched out a 2–1 win. It was as close as they would come. The Oilers won game four by the sizeable margin of 5–1, then polished off the Bruins 4–1 in game five to win their fifth Stanley Cup.

"This was a lot like the first year," said Messier. "It was like winning it for the first time all over again.

The event was noteworthy for one main reason: Edmonton had won the Stanley Cup without the Great One. In his place, Mark Messier, wearing the captain's "C," took the Cup from John Zeigler and hoisted it over his head while the fans in the Boston Garden applauded politely. Bill Ranford, who allowed only eight goals in five games of work between the pipes, was named the Conn Smythe Trophy winner as MVP of the playoffs.

But the summer that should have been one of celebration for the Oilers instead turned into another media event. Almost everyone had forgotten the 1986 *Sports Illustrated* article alleging that five members of the team had abused illegal drugs. The *Edmonton Journal* later learned and confirmed that one of those alleged players was Oilers goaltending sensation Grant Fuhr.

The *Journal* had confirmed the story through Fuhr's wife, Corrine, from whom he was currently estranged. Corrine told stories of Fuhr's binges and of having drug dealers show up at their home in the middle of the night demanding payment. Fuhr responded to the story by checking himself in to a drug treatment facility in Florida for the first few weeks of the NHL's 1990 season. Just weeks before the season got underway, the NHL, which at the time believed that drug abuse was less of a health concern and more of a character flaw, announced that Fuhr would be suspended for the duration of the 1990–91 season. Fuhr wasn't the only player missing that season. Winger Jari Kurri decided to play in Italy during the 1990–91 season.

While the Oilers players were distracted by Fuhr's battle with cocaine, Glen Sather was getting worried about his boss. Although he had eventually settled the Gainers strike years before, Pocklington had put the meatpacking plant up as collateral for a $55 million loan from the Alberta Treasury Branch. In 1989, Gainers defaulted on a series of loan payments due to the province under the terms of the 1987 agreement. When the money didn't arrive, the government sued Pocklington and started proceedings to take his beloved plant away from him.

The Oilers team that took to the ice for the 1990–91 season, though the defending Stanley Cup champions, were surrounded by distractions from both their boss and their star goaltender. Ranford was now the de facto starting goalie for Edmonton and played 60 games for the club, winning 27 and posting a 3.20 GAA. The team finished the season at 37–37–6, the first time the team had finished with a .500-or-below record since the early 1980s. Part of the reason for the slide revolved around its offensive production, or lack thereof. The 1991 Oilers scored only 272 goals, a far cry from their record-breaking output only a handful of years earlier. Esa Tikkanen led the team in scoring with 69 points, but Petr Klima, whose talent was always obfuscated by his "why should I bother" attitude, topped the Oilers in goal scoring with 40. Simpson potted 30 points, Anderson 24, and Mark Messier, who had missed 30 games due to injury, only 12. The team's scoring was a matter of concern, but their goaltending was not. John Zeigler lifted Fuhr's suspension after 60 games. In his first game back between the pipes, Fuhr posted a shutout in a 4–0 win over the New Jersey Devils.

Now armed with two Stanley Cup–winning goaltenders, the Oilers waded into the first round of the playoffs against the Calgary Flames, knowing this year's playoffs would be even more of a battle than the previous year's. The Oilers won three of the first four games to take a 3–1 lead in the series before Calgary battled back with 5–3 and 2–1 wins in games five and six to tie the series at three games apiece. The Oilers, however, squeaked out a 5–4 win in the deciding seventh game.

As they had the two seasons prior, the Oilers were also again condemned to play their old superstar Wayne Gretzky and his Los Angeles Kings. Although they dropped the first game by a score of 4–3, Edmonton went on a tear in games two, three and four, posting 4–3, 4–3 and 4–2 wins to take a 3–1 lead in the series. The Kings won game five by a 5–2 margin, but Edmonton sealed their round two victory with a 4–3 win in game six.

"Everybody in this room knows how to win a Stanley Cup," said Tikkanen, who scored a hat trick and the game-winning goal in game seven. "We know we can win the big games. We can do it. We've done it before."

If there was one team no one expected to be in
the Campbell Conference finals in 1991, it was the
Minnesota North Stars. Led by the surprising play
of small but agile goaltender John Casey, a man
who required 13 hours of sleep on game days to
get in the right frame of mind, the North Stars
were now making their first ever substantive
charge for the playoffs. The Oilers, as improbable
as it seemed, were trying to repeat as Stanley
Cup champions. The North Stars, proved to be
too strong and fast for the Oilers. They pasted
Minnesota in the series second game by a score
of 7–2 but lost games one, three, four and five
by a combined score of 18–7.

"We were out of gas," said Lowe. "Calgary and
Los Angeles took too much out of us."

It was the last series the North Stars would
win. They lost the Stanley Cup final to Mario
Lemieux's Pittsburgh Penguins, which also
featured former Oilers blueliner Paul Coffey in
their lineup. It wasn't even June, and the Oilers
were already finished playing for the season, all
except for two. Bill Ranford and Mark Messier
were the only Edmonton Oilers selected to play
on the 1991 Canada Cup squad, along with
former Oilers Wayne Gretzky and Paul Coffey.
Ranford won the starting job between the pipes
and guided the Canadian squad to a 6–0–2 finish,
which included winning both Cup final games

against the United States. Posting a 1.75 GAA in his eight games of work, Ranford was selected as the tournament's MVP.

Yet the Oilers' moves over the course of the summer did not bode well for the team. With Gretzky gone, every other Oiler who had been a part of the glory years of the 1980s was ready to strike out on his own. Everyone on the team could sense that the team was cracking, that its current chemistry was no longer good enough to guarantee any future success. Behind closed doors, Pocklington was trying to convince Glen Sather to tighten the team's belt and get rid of some of the players whose escalating salaries were eating away at what little capital he had left.

No sooner had the season ended for the Oilers than Sather began dismantling the team that he had spent more than 10 years building. Some may argue the bleeding well and truly started when Gretzky was traded to the Kings, but the summer and fall of 1991 proved to the entire hockey world that the dynasty days of the Edmonton Oilers were now officially over. On May 30, 1991, Sather traded the rights to Jari Kurri, who had been play-ing in Italy the previous season, along with Dave Brown and Corey Foster to the Philadelphia Flyers in exchange for Craig Fisher, Scott Mellanby and Craig Berube. The Flyers immediately flipped

Kurri to the Los Angeles Kings, where he was reunited with his old linemate Wayne Gretzky.

Training camp scarcely got underway when Sather pulled the trigger on another big trade, again depleting his team of its stalwart veterans. Slats packaged Glenn Anderson and Grant Fuhr together and shipped the pair to Toronto in exchange for talented centre Vincent Damphousse, Scott Thornton, tough defenceman Luke Richardson and backup goaltender Peter Ing. It was a chance for Anderson to play for a different team with a different style and also a chance for Fuhr to resurrect his career in a hockey environment that cared less about his past transgression than his play on the ice.

The bleeding continued when, less than two weeks after trading Anderson and Fuhr, Sather decided to trade his biggest bargaining chip yet. Mark Messier, who had succeeded Gretzky as the team's leader and who was one of the few remaining Oilers left from the dynasty days of the 1980s, decided that it was time to leave Edmonton, and he made it known during the Canada Cup. On October 4, 1991, Sather traded Messier to the New York Rangers in exchange for forward Bernie Nicholls, who had enjoyed several career years playing with Wayne Gretzky in Los Angeles before ending up on Broadway. As well, Steven Rice and tough but troubled enforcer Louis DeBrusk went to New York. Adam Graves also left for Manhattan, signing a $2.4 million contract after scoring seven goals for the Oilers. He went on to record one 50-goal season. John Muckler bolted from the bench for Buffalo, leaving Ted Green in charge.

Despite their completely revamped lineup, the Oilers still turned in a respectable 1991–92 season, finishing it with an above-.500 record (36–34–10) that was good enough for third place in the Smythe division. Newcomer Vincent Damphousse led the Oilers in scoring with 38 goals and 51 assists, while Joe Murphy finished second with 35 goals and 47 assists. No one else on the team scored more than 30 goals, though six other players on the team scored 20 or more: Craig Simpson (24), Scott Mellanby (23), Bernie Nicholls (20), Kelly Buchberger (20), Anatoli Semenov (20) and Petr Klima (21). Besides trading for Richardson, the Oilers beefed up the blueline by adding Blackhawks defenceman Dave Manson. Bill Ranford was again solid in net, playing 67 games and winning 27 while posting a 3.58 GAA. Peter Ing provided steady backup goaltending, but the Oilers eventually added former Québec Nordiques puckstopper Ron Tugnutt to the lineup to give Ranford a more reliable partner between the pipes.

The Oilers' third-place finish in the Smythe was good enough for them to qualify for the playoffs, during which, for the fourth year in a row, they faced the Los Angeles Kings. The first-round match up was another hotly contested affair, but the Oilers, who boasted more scoring depth through the forward lineups than the Kings, managed to control both Gretzky and Kurri in all six games. The teams traded victories through the first four games before Edmonton won game five by a score of 5–2. Ranford added a playoff shutout to his growing resume of accomplishments in game six when the Oilers won the game 3–0, clinching the series in six games.

The Smythe Division Finals featured a new opponent for the Oilers in post-season hockey: the Vancouver Canucks. After winning the first game 4–3, Canucks goaltender Kirk MacLean shut the door on the Edmonton Oilers in game two, blanking them 4–0. The Oilers responded with two straight victories, 5–2 and 3–2, both on home ice at Northlands Coliseum. The Canucks pushed the series to a sixth game with a 4–3 win at home, but the Oilers polished off their rivals from BC with another shutout victory, this time 3–0.

Fans and the media alike were talking about the Chicago Blackhawks as a team of destiny. Boasting Carmen, Manitoba, native Ed Belfour in net, and Steve Larmer, Jeremy Roenick and Chris Chelios on the ice, Chicago was seen as one of the teams with the best chance of preventing the Pittsburgh Penguins from repeating as Stanley Cup champions. The Oilers may not have agreed, but they could not get any rubber past Belfour. The Blackhawks swept the series in four games, winning by scores of 8–2, 4–2, 4–3 and 5–1. Even though they earned their birth in the Cup final, the Blackhawks fell before Lemieux's Penguins in four games.

"I'm really proud of what happened," said Green. "We came into a situation where nobody expected us to make the playoffs. It was total reorganization."

The Oilers had made it to the conference finals each of the last three years, winning the Stanley Cup once. It was an enviable record, considering the high rate of player turnover the players had experienced in the last two years.

But the next season, for the first time in its history in the NHL, the Edmonton Oilers missed the playoffs.

Chapter Six

The Long Way Down

If the Oilers' faithful had any doubts that the 1992–93 season would signal the beginning of Edmonton's "rebuilding years," the first dozen games of the regular season erased them completely.

The Oilers lost their first game of the season to the Vancouver Canucks team they had ousted the previous spring by a score of 5–4. In the first of the year's Battle of Alberta grudge matches, the Flames pounded Edmonton by a score of 7–2. Two nights later, the Oilers again took on the Canucks and lost, this time by a score of 5–2. They tied Toronto at home 3–3 the following night then dropped a 7–3 decision to the Winnipeg Jets. On October 15, the Oilers finally posted their first win of the season, beating Chicago 4–3 but went on to lose their next four games, starting the first eight games of the season with a record of 1–6–1. It was a telling sign to the entire hockey world that the Oilers were no longer the powerhouse they had once been. Their victory over Chicago was one of only 26 in total the team managed during the regular season, finishing with a record of 26–50–8, winning only half as many games as they lost.

As the Oilers continued to flail, Sather started making more changes to the lineup in the hopes of finding some sort of winning combination. On December 11, 1992, he dealt the Oilers' first-ever draft pick, Kevin Lowe, the man who had scored the team's first NHL goal, to the New York Rangers.

"I thought Kevin Lowe might be the one guy who was with us the whole way," said Sather.

In the New Year, Sather flipped centre Vincent Damphousse to the Montréal Canadiens in exchange for pesky winger Shane Corson, defenceman Brent Gilchrist and prospect Vladimir Vujtek. At the trade deadline, Sather kept the bodies moving, trading holdout forward Joe Murphy to Chicago for talented forward Igor Kravchuk and speedy centre Dean McAmmond. He also dealt perennial pest and team leader Esa Tikkanen to the New York Rangers for a young American centre named Doug Weight, who managed eight points in the 13 games he spent with Edmonton. None of the trades were enough to pull the Oilers up out of their season-long funk. When spring rolled around, the Oilers found themselves on the outside of the playoff picture looking in. They watched as former teammates Wayne Gretzky and Marty McSorley went on to challenge the Montréal Canadiens in the Stanley Cup final but ultimately lose.

"If the idea is to make the playoffs every year in history, blame me," said Sather. "Sure, we thought we could do it. But there was no way I was going to try it any other way."

No one really knew who Joe Hulbig was. The Oilers had drafted him with their first-round selection in 1992, but he quickly proved that he was going to be another one of the Oilers' perennial draft busts. 1993 proved to be a much more promising year. Slated to pick sixth over-all, Glen Sather stepped to the podium and announced the Oilers were selecting Oshawa Generals centre Jason Arnott. The Collingwood, Ontario, centre had gone from scoring nine goals and 15 assists in his first year with the Generals to posting 41 goals and 57 assists in his second year. The Oilers were banking on Arnott to step into the lineup as soon as possible to help bolster an offence that was now lacking in production.

In the fifth round of the draft, Sather struck again with another successful selection, picking Slovakian-born left winger Miroslav Satan with the 111th selection. Playing in the Czech Republic, the six-foot-tall winger had scored 11 goals and

6 assists in 38 games. He went on to increase his point total six-fold in the following year with 42 goals and 22 assists.

The draft proved rich for other reasons as well. Although they didn't know it at the time, nine of the players selected that year would go on to wear Oilers jerseys at some point in their career.

With Arnott secure and ready for camp, Sather decided to do some serious house cleaning in the hopes of kick-starting the team into the 1993–94 campaign. Bernie Nicholls had already been traded, sent to New Jersey in exchange for Zdeno Ciger and Kevin Todd. In June, Slats finally rid the team of perennial underachiever Petr Klima by sending him to Tampa Bay in exchange for a third-round draft pick in 1994.

"Petr's been a coach-killer wherever he's been," said coach Ted Green. "I don't give a damn about Petr Klima. I've run out of patience. Here's a guy who only cares about himself."

Sather followed up by trading Martin Gelinas and a sixth round pick to the Québec Nordiques for Scott Pearson, then dealt Craig Simpson to Buffalo in exchange for Jozef Cierny and a fourth round draft pick in 1994.

The season had barely started when Sather flipped Kevin Todd to the Blackhawks in exchange for Adam Bennett. One month later he traded Chris Joseph to Tampa Bay for Bob Beers, then a month after that traded Geoff Smith and a fourth round pick in 1994 to the Florida Panthers in exchange for their third and sixth round picks.

At first, it seemed as if the Oilers might have found a winning solution. They won their first game of the season against San Jose by a score of 3–2 before pasting the New York Islanders 5–1. Two nights later, the Vancouver Canucks dealt Edmonton their first loss of the season. It was the start of a streak in which the Oilers won only one of their next 14 games, which included a jaw-dropping 11-game losing streak. After the woeful start reached the 3–18–3 mark, Sather supplanted Green behind the bench and tried to steer the team out of the muck.

"I'm not happy with what happened today. I recognize the crowds were getting smaller and we were dropping lower and lower in the standings. If we had more scoring, all this would be academic. But I'm the guy who was responsible and accountable," said Green.

Sather continued to pull the trigger on the trading gun, acquiring defenceman Fredrick Olausson from the Winnipeg Jets for a draft pick then trading Marc Laforge to the Islanders for Brent Grieve. In March, Sather traded Brad Werenka to the Nordiques for prospect goalie

Steve Passmore, then packaged Dave Manson with a sixth round pick to Winnipeg in exchange for a first and fourth round pick, plus forward prospect Mats Lindgren and rookie defenceman Boris Mironov. He also dispatched long-time Oiler Craig MacTavish to the New York Rangers for a young, speedy forward named Todd Marchant. By season's end, the Oilers had only managed 25 wins, while losing 45 and tying 14. It was their worst season to date and, for the second year in a row, the Oilers failed to make the playoffs.

There were, of course, individual successes to celebrate. In his first full year with the Oilers, centre Doug Weight led the team in scoring with 24 goals and 50 assists. More remarkable still was the success of rookie forward Jason Arnott. The first-round draft pick turned in a stellar first year, scoring 33 goals and adding 35 assists. Only Arnott, Weight, Ciger and Corson, however, breached the 20-goal plateau. Seven players on the team recorded 10 goals or more as the Oilers offence continued to slump heavily. Ranford continued to be the Oilers' best player night in and night out, playing 71 games, winning 22 and posting a 3.48 GAA and respectable .898 save percentage.

Rather than competing for the Stanley Cup, the Oilers were forced to sit back and watch the

New York Rangers, featuring Mark Messier, Craig MacTavish, Kevin Lowe, Esa Tikkanen, Glenn Anderson, Adam Graves and Jeff Beukeboom, come out and beat the Vancouver Canucks for the Stanley Cup. Messier won the Conn Smythe trophy as the playoffs' most valuable player, while Wayne Gretzky again captured the league scoring title. All the ex-Oilers it seemed were succeeding in their lives after Edmonton. It was the current Oilers that were having the most trouble.

The National Hockey League as a whole was also in trouble. The entire 1993–94 year had been played without a collective bargaining agreement in place. Negotiations seemed to be going nowhere and though training camps opened in September, the owners locked out the NHL's 600 players on October 1 in an effort to get the NHL Players' Association (NHLPA) to negotiate on its terms. Salaries were exploding as players found they could now market themselves to the teams willing to pay them the most money. The average salary had quickly surpassed the $1 million mark in just a few years since the players' 10-day walkout in 1992. The salary peaks were affecting small-market teams such as Edmonton, Québec and Winnipeg that simply didn't have the marketing base from which to draw on millions of dollars. The owners wanted to institute some kind of salary cap that would put a limit on how much teams could spend on salaries.

The NHL also wanted to tie salaries to revenues to try to help subsidize the operations of weaker teams. The NHLPA steadfastly refused to consider the possibility. As the months crept by, it began to look increasingly as though the 1994–95 season might never start.

On January 11, 1995, the two sides finally came to an agreement. The only salary cap instituted was on rookie salaries, but those were easily worked around using a succession of performance bonuses. The negotiations also made salary arbitration non-binding and eliminated Group I free agency. The owners honestly believed at the time that limiting the amount of money a rookie could make in his first few years would help smaller market teams save money.

The hockey season, however, was already practically half over. The NHL quickly introduced a 48-game schedule, a veritable sprint to the playoffs. The Oilers were ready for the sprint that started on January 20, 1995, sporting a new coach behind the bench. Sather had promoted George Burnett, coach of the team's AHL affiliate Cape Breton Oilers, to the head coaching position. Burnett had taken Cape Breton to the Calder Cup in 1993 and came to Edmonton with the hopes of turning the team's losing ways around.

"When I took over this team 17 years ago, I was the same age as this guy," said Sather when he introduced Burnett.

No one knew whether it was the shortened schedule or the coach himself, but Burnett had little or no influence on the Oilers' performance on the ice. By the time the first 35 games were played, the Oilers had won only 12 of them. Burnett and Shayne Corson were also feuding openly, which contributed to the team's poor efforts on the ice. Burnett stripped Corson of the captain's "C" only seven games after giving it to him. On April 6, Sather fired Burnett, appointing Ron Low in his place.

"The dressing room was in chaos," said Sather. "Whether they'll play for you is the most important part. I blame myself. George is going to be a good coach, but with this group, it wasn't working."

Low was one of the first former players to prove the now time-honoured axiom that old Oilers never leave Edmonton. The former netminder played for the Oilers for three years, from 1980 to 1983, before being traded to New Jersey. He spent time coaching in Cape Breton before becoming an assistant coach with Edmonton in 1989. Low was brash and determined, and the players responded with a slightly better effort, winning five of their last 13 games. Doug Weight led the team again in scoring with 40 points, while Arnott chipped in 37 and Corson 36. Ranford won 15 of 40 starts, but his GAA ballooned to 3.68. The team's final record of 17–27–4 was not enough to make the playoffs, and for the third season in a row, the Oilers were forced to watch the playoffs rather than play in them.

The lockout-shortened season was a sad yet important one for the NHL. Two of Canada's former teams were essentially prepared to cease operations. The Québec Nordiques, who had long been playing out of the dilapidated La Colisée in Québec City, were denied money for a new rink from both the city and province and were instead sold to Denver and became the Colorado Avalanche.

The Winnipeg Jets were being moved to Phoenix where they would become the Coyotes for the start of the 1996–97 season. Two of the small-market teams the NHL had tried to save were now moving to bigger markets because there was just not enough financial parity in the league for them to remain in Canada.

The Oilers started to feel the financial pinch as well. Regular season attendance began to drop steadily once the Oilers started missing the playoffs, because fans found they only enjoyed watching their team play when they were winning. On some nights, the attendance

numbered fewer than 10,000 fans, no matter what the public relations staff at the game
announced. The Oilers did not have a major cable
network deal and did not have an owner with
unlimited financial resources. Consequently,
the Oilers could not afford to pay the big name
salaries that were becoming increasingly com-
mon in the NHL. If the Oilers were ever going
to be a winning team again, they were going to
have to grow their talent, not trade for it.

There was room for at least one marquee
player in the lineup. That spot was reserved for
the goaltender. During the off-season Sather
sent St. Louis the Oilers' first-round picks in the
1996 and 1997 drafts for forward Mike Grier
and promising goaltender Curtis Joseph. Joseph
decided to spend the first half of the season playing in Las Vegas until he could negotiate a new
deal with the Oilers. With Edmonton again floundering in the regular season, Sather convinced
Joseph to play for the Oilers. In response, Sather
traded Ranford back to the Boston team he had
originally been acquired from, receiving forward
Mariusz Czerkawski, defenceman Sean Brown
and a first-round draft pick in 1996.

The Oilers still missed the playoffs, but their
record was better than in the preceding three
years at 30–44–8. "CuJo," as Joseph was affec-
tionately known in the NHL, started 34 games

for the Oilers, winning 15 of them and posting a 3.44 GAA. Doug Weight broke the 100-point plateau with 25 goals and 79 assists. Zdeno Ciger potted 31 goals, while Arnott continued to impress with 28 goals and 31 assists in 80 games. Forward Miroslav Satan, who had been selected in the same draft year as Arnott, also scored in a respectable 18 goals and 17 assists in 62 games of work, while the incredibly speedy but cement-handed Todd Marchant potted 19 goals of his own.

The resurgence in the Oilers towards the end of the season was enough to again pique fans' interest. During the summer, the NHL announced that the Oilers absolutely had to sell 13,000 season tickets for 1996–97 or the team would have to be moved. The fans responded, snapping up as many tickets as they could in order to keep the team in Edmonton. After all, the Oilers had a brand new goaltender and a lineup that looked as though it might actually be able to win a few games in the year ahead. Northlands Coliseum was also looking pretty good, having undergone a multimillion-dollar retrofit and renovation that added much-needed luxury box revenue to the team's financial portfolio.

The team continued its lengthy hit-and-miss streak at the annual amateur entry draft, and it mostly missed. With its first pick in the 1994 draft, fourth overall, the Oilers selected Jason Bonsignore from the Niagara Falls Thunder of the OHL. Fortunately for the Oilers, they had one more pick in the first round, sixth overall. Sather decided to look in his own backyard and called the name of Ryan Smyth, who had played the previous season with the Moose Jaw Warriors of the WHL. Born in Banff, Alberta, Smyth was a left winger known for his work ethic and durability. In his draft year he scored 50 goals and added 55 assists while racking up 88 penalty minutes. His specialty was setting up in the opponent's slot, screening the goaltender and scoring on deflections or rebound garbage goals that no other player wanted.

The 1995 draft was even more sparse for the Oilers, who took left winger Steve Kelly from the Prince Albert Raiders. In the second round Edmonton keyed in on Georges Laraques, a 6'3", 230-pound behemoth left winger who played for the St. Jeans Lynx. In his draft year, Laraques scored 19 goals and 22 assists in 61 games while compiling 259 penalty minutes. Laraques was more of an enforcer than a goon, but the Oilers were in need of someone who was willing to mix it up when the going got tough.

The 1996 entry draft was a little deeper for the team in that some of the players selected actually saw some playing time with the big team.

The Oilers selected Boyd Devereaux in the first round, a centre with the Kitchener Rangers who scored 20 goals and 38 assists in 66 games. In the fifth round, the Oilers selected U.S. defenceman Tom Poti, a gifted offensive defenceman.

In the eighth round, the Oilers again looked close to home and took one of the most distinctive players in the draft. With its 195th selection, the Oilers picked 20-year-old left winger Fernando Pisani, an Edmonton native who had grown up in the city's Little Italy. The six-foot forward was playing in the Alberta Junior Hockey League for the St. Albert Saints. In 1996–97, Pisani moved on to college hockey in the U.S., where he played for Providence College, scoring 30, 34, 51 and 38 points during the NCAA 36-game seasons in all four years he attended.

The Oilers team that greeted the beginning of the 1996–97 season finally looked like they were a team set for the future. They had a leader in Doug Weight, strong goaltending in Curtis Joseph and young talent toiling away in the minors.

The only question to be answered was whether the team would be playing in Edmonton or in some other new city.

Chapter Seven

The "Puck" Stops Here

The Oilers weren't just struggling on the ice in the early 1990s. Not a day went by when the people of Edmonton weren't faced with the possibility that they might lose their NHL team.

Peter Pocklington was in dire financial straits. The Gainers strike had cost him a significant amount of capital, and the province was now starting to make noise about the $55 million loan it had given him through the Alberta Treasury Branch. Gainers had defaulted on the loan back in 1990, and the province was looking to seize Gainers from Pocklington, which the Oilers' owner had put up as collateral for his loan. Suits and countersuits flew back and forth as Pocklington tried to stave off the inevitable.

By 1992, Pocklington was already starting to grumble and complain publicly about the terms of his lease with Northlands. Under the agreement, Pocklington paid Northlands approximately

$2.3 million per year, yet he didn't receive any additional revenues from Northlands for having the Oilers play there, such as receipts from parking at Oilers games or a share of the concession sales. Northlands responded in February 1993 by offering to buy the team from Pocklington, offering the Oilers' owner $65 million. Pocklington brushed the offer aside and countered with a $105 million deal of his own. Northlands rejected the counteroffer. By April, Pocklington stated that unless a new lease was worked out in which he received a portion of the parking and concession revenues, he would move the team to Hamilton.

Hamilton was more than happy to entertain the offer. The city had been in the running for a franchise in the expansion bonanza that saw San Jose, Tampa Bay, Ottawa and Florida land NHL franchises. The city had been turned down because of its small market and its proximity to Buffalo and Toronto. Putting a team in Hamilton could deny both cities fans if Hamilton was given its own franchise.

Minneapolis was also making its intentions known of landing an NHL team. The city had bid farewell to the North Stars, who had moved to Dallas rather than continue to play in Minnesota. Faced with the threat of having one of the city's most important capital and tourist draws simply pull up stakes and leave, Edmonton decided to sit down and negotiate with Pocklington. In May, Economic Development Edmonton (EDE) worked out a deal with him in which the city paid the lease to Northlands, then sublet the Coliseum to Pocklington. The new lease also guaranteed Pocklington a share of parking and concession revenues.

The deal didn't last. Pocklington refused to guarantee that he would never try to move the team out of Edmonton, and Northlands was looking for a way to get a few million out of Pocklington. Only weeks after concluding the arrangement, the deal fell through. Soon afterwards, when the idea of moving the team to Minneapolis became public, the city went to court and successfully applied for an injunction that would prevent Pocklington from moving the team.

The federal government eventually swooped in with a $15 million grant that the city could use to renovate Northlands Coliseum, which was now approaching its 20th birthday. EDE used the receipt of the grant to resurrect the failed lease agreement of 1993, which Pocklington agreed to for a period of 10 years. Pocklington could also, with a few exceptions, charge rent to any group that wanted to rent Northlands. The city also put its support behind a new baseball stadium for the Edmonton Trappers, which Pocklington also owned.

Yet Pocklington's constant threat of moving the team if he didn't start making more money was not the only way Edmonton could lose the Oilers. The Alberta Treasury Branch was keeping a close eye on all of Pocklington's finances as he struggled to repay the $55 million loan. If at any time the province felt that Pocklington would be unable to repay the loan, they could seize all of his assets, including the Oilers, and sell them off to the highest bidder to pay off his debts. Pocklington had further increased his debt loan by sinking an estimated $15 million into the Northlands renovations and construction of Telus Field for his Trappers. If the province forced Pocklington to sell the team, he could do so to anyone who had the money to take it over: where they were from or what they planned to do with the team was irrelevant.

Therefore, EDE continued negotiating with Pocklington to try to guarantee the Oilers' survival in Edmonton. What ensued was the 1994 Location Agreement between the city and Pocklington that essentially gave EDE and Northlands the right to veto any decision to sell the Oilers or move them out of town. The agreement was to last for 10 years, meaning the Oilers had to stay in Edmonton until at least 2004. The agreement also guaranteed that, in the event the Alberta Treasury Branch forced Pocklington to sell the team, the city would have 30 days to come up with a local buyer for the team. The parties also negotiated a maximum sale price for a local owner: anyone wanting first dibs on the Oilers would have to shell out $70 million to buy the team from Pocklington. If no one came forward with the money in the 30 days specified in the agreement, either Pocklington or the Alberta Treasury Branch was free to sell the team to the next highest bidder, regardless of where they were from.

The four-month lockout that delayed the start of the 1994–95 season meant that Pocklington had to go four months with very little revenue coming in from Northlands' principle tenant, the Edmonton Oilers. The declining attendance at the Oilers games when the season did resume also deprived him of much-needed capital that was intended to go towards servicing his debts. Missing the playoffs for four straight years also hit Pocklington hard in the wallet—he maintained that he personally lost $3.5 million in the 1996–97 campaign. By 1997, it was clear to both the city and to the Alberta Treasury Branch that Pocklington could no longer pay his debts. They started going after all of his assets, which included the Oilers, the Trappers, a controlling share of Canbra foods, the Edmonton Drillers of the National Professional Soccer League, as well as some private real estate holdings. Pocklington had to start looking for a buyer before the Alberta Treasury Branch forced him to sell off the team on their terms instead of his.

The team's first prospective buyer was Leslie Alexander, a former trader who was now interested in owning sports teams. He owned the Houston Rockets of the NBA, as well as an Arena Football League Team and a Women's NBA team. Houston had been on the list of cities considered for expansion NHL franchises but was left off the final list that included Nashville, Atlanta, St. Paul and Columbus. Rather than sit and fret, Alexander looked north. Instead of asking the NHL for a franchise, it just might work better to buy an existing franchise and move it to town.

That franchise was the Edmonton Oilers, though Alexander had an idea going in that simply stealing the Oilers away from the city was going to be difficult. He told the *Edmonton Journal* in an October 24 story that he was ready to let the Oilers continue to play in Edmonton for the time being, so long as it proved profitable. If there was no money to be had as a result of the deal, then Alexander would have no choice but to move them. After all, he was first and foremost a businessman who was concerned with making money, not losing it.

On November 3, Alexander arrived in Edmonton to sit down and discuss the potential deal with Mayor Bill Smith and the head of EDE. Smith was less than enthusiastic about Alexander's ideas. The meeting between the mayor and the Texan lasted less than half an hour, during which time Smith explained to Alexander exactly what the Location Agreement was and how it worked. Alexander stated furiously that he had no intention of signing off on the agreement, apparently because Pocklington had misled him about how serious the city took the agreement. Alexander drove immediately from city hall to the airport and returned to Houston.

Alexander was confident that he could work his way around the Location Agreement. In his mind, the Location Agreement was a non-starter that he could easily backdate and step around to a point where he could pluck the Oilers out of the city, if he so chose. On February 10, 1998, Alexander made an official offer to Peter Pocklington to buy the Oilers for $82.5 million. The offer officially triggered the purchase clause in the Location Agreement, which gave any local bidders 30 days to buy the team for $70 million. Of that $70 million, however, only half of the cost could be financed, according to league rules. The other half had to come from straight capital investment by the prospective owner.

The rallying cry went out to the city: save our Oilers, and the business community slowly began to respond. Lawyer Cal Nichols led the charge, burning up his Rolodex contacting local investors to try to sell them on the idea. It was obvious from the start that there was no single person who could step in and rescue the Oilers. Although a prosperous city and the provincial capital, Edmonton was not a serious economic hot bed. It was an oil town to be sure, but the bigger oil town was three hours to the south, where most of the big companies operated. Any effort would have to involve securing a coalition of owners who were willing to sink some portion of their capital into the venture and effectively share the team. After the first week of calling and soliciting, Nichols drummed up 13 investors who were to collectively chip in $28 million. Edmonton was now short a minimum of $7 million in order to get the NHL to even think about letting the team stay in the city.

What followed was one of the strangest stories in the history of team ownership in the NHL. With the first week gone and the hopes of an entire city resting on the goodwill of local businesses, the people of Edmonton were willing to listen to anyone who could help keep the Oilers in town. Without warning, a man from New York City called EDE, saying he had some money that he was willing to use to buy the Oilers outright, more so, if a deal could be reached that was favourable to him. And he had every intention of leaving the Oilers in Edmonton.

The man's name was Michael Largue, and not only did he offer his own money to buy the team, but also the finances of a friend in Switzerland who was the former president of the Credite Suisse bank. Both the city and the media immediately jumped on the opportunity, and Largue quickly hopped aboard the next plane to Edmonton. The city did a perfunctory check of Largue's background and declared him legitimate. It rolled out the red carpet for Largue, ready to treat him as a white knight.

According to Largue, he was a devoted hockey fan and a former hockey player. He claimed to have played hockey at Northeastern University and briefly with the Bern Bears of the Swiss Elite League. It was during his time in Switzerland that he met Leslie Mittendorf, the Swiss banker who he said had owned the Bern Bears when Largue had played there.

The city assumed that both Largue and his money were legit, and the local fundraising process ground to a halt while the city awaited Largue's arrival. Yet the more the local media started digging into Largue's past, the more it found that parts of Largue's story didn't add up. The *Edmonton Journal* placed a call to Northeastern University to confirm that Largue had played there, but according to them, there was no record of a Michael Largue ever playing for their team. More puzzling still, the university did not have a record of ever having a Michael Largue enrolled at their school. The *Edmonton Journal* continued following up the story, contacting the Bern Bears of the Swiss Elite League. The team had no record of anyone named Michael Largue playing for them. There was also no record in all of Switzerland of anyone by the name of Leslie Mittendorf ever being president of Credite Suisse or owning the Bern Bears.

Largue had no sooner arrived in Edmonton and introduced himself to the local media than the *Journal* pressed him for answers. The revelations came as a shock to Largue and the city officials and representatives of the investors group who were scheduled to show Largue around the city, including a tour of Northlands Coliseum. Largue provided no explanations for the inconsistencies, and by the time he arrived at Northlands, it was easy to tell that the city was no longer interested in dealing with him.

The episode was as much of an embarrassment for Edmonton and its group of would-be investors as it had been for Largue himself. Although they claimed to have checked Largue's references, it was difficult to believe that anyone who had bothered to look into the white knight's past could have overlooked some of the glaring inconsistencies the *Journal* had uncovered. By the end of the day, Largue was back on a plane, beating a hasty retreat from the City of Champions. The city was left foaming at the mouth, having wasted an entire week courting Largue—precious time that could have been used to find more local investors.

The strange nature of the story did not stop there. As the *Journal* continued to dig into Largue's past, they found out more about who this man was and what kinds of things he had done in his past. The previous March, Largue had been charged with fraud for misappropriating funds at an apartment co-op in the U.S. He was convicted and was living at home with his parents when he called the Oilers and made his offer. By coming to Edmonton, he had actually violated the terms of his probation.

It also turned out this was not the first time Largue had pulled a similar stunt. He had twice made offers to buy the Hartford Whalers, once in 1994 and again in 1997 with the goal of keeping the team in Connecticut. One month after blasting the Whalers' owner for moving the team from Hartford to Raleigh, North Carolina, Largue approached the Tampa Bay Lightning and inquired about the possibility of buying the team. The Lightning, unlike the Oilers, did their due diligence and checked into Largue's background. They never heard from him again.

With only days left to spare before Leslie Alexander's offer would win out over their own, the Edmonton investors group got back to work, again pressing local businesses for their support. The *Edmonton Journal* surprised everyone by stepping in with a $1 million donation, which it stated it would sell once the team was officially sold to the new group. Car dealer Ron Hodgson was one of the group of 13 already on board, along with former president of the CFL's Edmonton Eskimos, Jim Hole, and Bruce Saville, president of Saville Systems. Slowly, the push gained momentum. Barry Weaver, owner of Skyreach Equipment in St. Albert, pledged another $1 million while notable comic book artist Todd McFarlane, creator of the hit comic series *Spawn*, also chipped in to the venture. By the time March 12 arrived, almost 30 days after Alexander had first triggered the clause in the Location Agreement, the group had managed to secure the minimum $35 million in capital needed to keep the team in town.

Days after pooling the final total, the investors group successfully secured a $35 million loan from the Bank of Nova Scotia to cover the remainder of the cost of the team. On March 18, the Alberta Treasury Branch gave the investors group the final okay to complete the transaction and officially relieve Peter Pocklington of his burdensome hockey team. After a short meeting with the NHL to trumpet the merits of the new deal, the investors group sat down with the city and Northlands to arrange a new lease. Under the new deal, the investors group leased the Coliseum from Northlands for $1 per year but still received concession revenues from Oilers games and a healthy portion of parking revenues. Northlands also sold off the naming rights to the Coliseum for an estimated $1 million. The lucky buyer was one of the group's own. Barry Weaver promptly rechristened the Coliseum as Skyreach Centre and affixed a blazing, neon-lit copy of his company's logo on the building to advertise it as such. The new lease, however, left Northlands almost $5 million in the whole. It was willing eat half of the cost, but only if the city came up with the rest. On April 25, Edmonton city council approved a $2.4 million operating grant for Northlands to subsidize those losses.

There was only one thing left to wait for, and it came quickly. On April 27, the NHL officially gave its blessing to the sale of the Edmonton Oilers to the investors group. The city celebrated because this deal, unlike any of the others, guaranteed the once formidable dynasty would remain in Edmonton for years to come. Peter Pocklington was effectively shunted off to the sidelines and quickly forgotten. After six years of listening to the entrepreneur complain about how the city was treating him and his team, the people of Edmonton wanted nothing more to do with him. They never wanted to hear another word about leases, Location Agreements and phantom buyers from other cities.

The people of Edmonton were ready to sit down and watch some hockey.

Chapter Eight

The Long Road to Dallas

It almost looked as if the 1996–97 Oilers, aware of the precarious state of the team, were trying to market themselves to whichever new owner or city decided to take them on.

When the season opened in October, the team seemed to decide that enough was enough; it was time to make hockey in Edmonton exciting again. In the first six games, the Oilers went 4–1–1, their best start since their last playoff performance. Joseph provided the anchor the Oilers needed in goal while young defenceman Boris Mironov patrolled the bluelines with veteran Kevin Lowe, who returned to the team to finish up his playing days. Up front, Doug Weight led a revamped Oilers offence that quickly proved itself as one of the fastest in the NHL. The Oilers weren't always perfect but scarcely a game went by where TV and radio commentators weren't mentioning the speed of the entire Oilers team.

Despite the 4–1–1 start, the Oilers still struggled through the season. On November 9, they posted a 6–0 win over the Boston Bruins. Two days later, they lost 7–2 to the Toronto Maple Leafs. They lost 7–3 to Dallas on November 17 but pounded Calgary 10–1 less than one week later. Every promising step forward was accompanied by a reluctant step backward. The steps forward, however, kept them in pace with the top teams in the NHL. By the time the season ended on April 12, 1997, the Oilers still didn't have a winning record. The team finished the season with a 36–37–9 record, but their point total was good enough to vault the team into the post-season.

"I see a young team getting better," said Joseph. "I see a team developing a strong belief now that we're going to be a very tough team in the playoffs."

Joseph was a rock in goal, starting 72 games and posting a 2.93 GAA with 32 wins and six shutouts. Determined to shore up their netminding, the Oilers also added former Winnipeg Jets starting goaltender Bob Essensa, known to the rest of world as "Goalie Bob." In 19 games, Essensa also posted a diminutive 2.83 GAA.

Weight led the Oilers offence again with 21 goals and 61 assists. The real surprise came from a sophomore Alberta boy whose heart proved to be as big as his nose. Ryan Smyth, an Oilers draft pick, had played in 48 games the previous season, scoring only two goals and nine assists. In 1996–97, however, he caught fire. Playing in all 82 games, the second-year forward scored 39 goals and assisted on 22 others. Andrei Kovalenko added another 32 goals, while winger Mariusz Czerkawski finished the year with 26.

The Oilers were not given much of a chance going into the playoffs. Their first-round opponents were the Dallas Stars, who had finished the year tied for second place in the league, with 107 points.

The first game in Dallas started on a positive note for the Oilers. Todd Marchant, dubbed one of the fastest players in the NHL, scored the first goal of the game to give Edmonton a 1–0 lead. Dallas responded with a brilliant effort, holding the Oilers to only two more goals to take the first game by a final score of 5–3. Edmonton regrouped and came out firing in game two, scoring four goals while Curtis Joseph effectively slammed the door on the Stars offence. The 4–0 victory was marred by an incident in which Bryan Marchment tripped over Dallas Stars forward Guy Carbonneau, ploughing head first into the door hinge of the penalty box and immediately going into convulsions. Although he was taken to hospital, Marchment was eventually cleared medically to return to the Oilers.

With five minutes left to go in game number three, the Oilers' hopes for a good playoff run didn't look promising. The Stars were up 3–0 and pressing hard, looking to take a 2–1 lead in the series. Doug Weight scored, which ruined former Oilers' netminder Andy Moog's shutout bid. Then Andrei Kovalenko scored, cutting the lead to one goal. Suddenly, Mike Grier added a third. The Oilers had tied the game in exactly one minute and 56 seconds. The crowds at Northlands went crazy, and that energy infected the rest of the team. At the 9:56 mark of overtime, Kelly Buchberger scored the winning goal, giving the Oilers one of their most exciting wins in their entire history thus far.

"What that does for your team is indescribable. You couldn't write a better script than that," said Weight.

The Stars thundered back in game four, taking the game 4–3. The teams fought to a 0–0 tie in game five before Ryan Smyth scored the winning goal in the second overtime period to give the Oilers a 3–2 lead in the series. Dallas, however, etched out a 3–2 win in game six to force an all-deciding seventh game. After 60 minutes of play, the Oilers and Stars were tied at 3–3, heading into overtime. At the 12:26 mark,

Todd Marchant, the man who had opened the series' scoring, also scored the last goal as he pulled away from the Stars defence and scored on a breakaway.

"I couldn't be more proud," said Sather.

If the Stars were a mountain to climb, then the Colorado Avalanche would be a veritable Mount Everest. The Avalanche lineup featured Stanley Cup–winning goalie Patrick Roy, sniper Joe Sakic, all-star Peter Forsberg and fast-skating Sandis Ozolinsh. Despite the Oilers' enthusiasm and effort, the Avalanche was just too much for them to handle. Edmonton managed to win game three by a 4–3 score on home ice, but the Avalanche won the first two and last two games of the series to advance to the conference final against Detroit.

The Oilers were good but not quite good enough to really make a run for a strong playoff position. That was obvious when the 1997–98 season began, and they started off the season with a 3–6–1 record in their first 10 games. With the team fighting to stay in contention, Sather decided to shake up the lineup a little bit and did so in a way that many fans publicly thanked him for. On January 4, 1998, Sather packaged Jason Arnott, whose offensive spark had dwindled and who was now openly reviled in the city, with Bryan Muir and shipped them to New Jersey for forwards Bill Guerin and Valeri Zelepukin. Sather also traded the ever-pesky Bryan Marchment to Tampa Bay in exchange for Roman Hamrlik, a solid blueliner with a nose for the net. The trades had their desired effect. On January 7, the Oilers beat the Florida Panthers 4–2. The team won its next five games, one of the longest winning streaks in recent history, which vaulted the Oilers back into the playoff race.

Although not quite as good as its record the previous season, Edmonton's 35–37–10 record was still good enough to get the team into the playoffs. That the Oilers played in the post-season at all was more a testament to Curtis Joseph's goaltending than to the team's offensive production. Joseph compiled eight shutouts and a 2.63 GAA in 71 games of work. Only two Oilers— Doug Weight (26) and Ryan Smyth (20)—scored more than 20 goals. Defenceman Boris Mironov was the team's third-leading scorer, with 16 goals and 30 assists. And the new players injected some life into the team. Bill Guerin scored 29 points in 40 games as an Oiler, while Hamrlik finished with 26 points in 41 games.

"I think Dallas last year was surprised by us," said Sather. "I don't think they expected us to be so gritty or determined. This time whoever we play will be aware of us. We're going to get a lot more respect than last year."

The Oilers' first-round challengers were the same Colorado Avalanche team that had bounced them from the playoffs the year before. Edmonton was determined to exact some measure of revenge. The Oilers rebounded from a 2–0 deficit in game one, scoring three goals in less than four minutes to win game one 3–2. Coach Ron Low pulled Curtis Joseph in game two after the netminder gave up four goals, and the Avalanche went on to a 5–2 win. Colorado leapt ahead of the Oilers in the series in games three and four, winning a close one, 5–4, in overtime followed by a more convincing 3–1 win in game four. Curtis Joseph took a lot of heat because of his less than stellar play, but the Edmonton netminder stepped up and played hard. In the ensuing three games, CuJo posted a microscopic 0.33 GAA, surrendering only one goal and shutting out the Avalanche twice. The Oilers won game five 3–1, game six 2–0 and shutout Colorado 3–0 in game seven to win the series.

"We wore 'em down," said Kelly Buchberger. "We could see we were wearing them out as the series went along. We wore them out."

In what would become an annual waltz through the NHL post-season, the Oilers again drew the Dallas Stars on their dance card. This year's Stars team, however, was not nearly so willing to let the Oilers run over them as they had the year before. The Stars won the first game 3–1, but in a defensive tour de force, the Oilers prevented the Stars from getting a shot on goal in the first period of game two. CuJo rode the tight defensive play to a 2–0 shutout win that tied the series at one game apiece. It was the last win for the Oilers. Benoit Hogue broke a 0–0 tie in overtime of game three to give the Stars the win. Dallas followed that up with a 3–1 win in game four and a 2–1 win in game five to take the series in five games.

They had made it to the second round of the playoffs, but the Oilers were playing the collective bargaining equivalent of Russian roulette with their star player. Rather than trade CuJo in the hopes of getting something for him before the playoffs began, the Oilers instead chose to ride him into the playoffs, even though his contract was due to expire at the end of the season. With a payroll budget of barely $25 million, one of the lowest in the NHL, the Oilers couldn't afford to give CuJo the money that he wanted to stay in Edmonton, and Joseph wasn't ready to take a pay cut to stay. In what would become an ongoing trend for Edmonton, the fans watched as Joseph signed a lucrative multi-year deal with the Toronto Maple Leafs.

To try to fill the gap left in net by Joseph's departure, Sather signed Goalie Bob to a one-year deal and traded goaltending prospect Eric Fichaud and defencemen Drake Berehowsky and Greg Devries to the Nashville Predators for netminder Mikhail Shtalenkov. He signed Ryan Smyth to a new contract but watched as Doug Weight sat out the first part of the season in a contract dispute. Despite these changes, the Oilers started strong, winning 6 of their first 10 games. A seven-game losing streak that started in December relegated the team to the back of the playoff race. Their record at the end of the year was again worse than it had been the year before, finishing at 33–37–12.

With Doug Weight holding out, then injured after he re-signed with the team, Bill Guerin picked up the leadership role on offence, scoring 30 goals and adding 34 assists. Josef Beranek chipped in 19 goals, while Mike Grier popped 20 goals and 24 assists. Former San Jose first rounder Pat Falloon added another 16 goals, and centre Rem Murray banged home 20. Mironov again led the blueliners in scoring with 11 goals and 29 assists.

The story between the pipes, however, was cause for concern. Essensa was getting older, and Shtalenkov's play was inconsistent. Essensa won 12 of 39 starts while Shtalenkov won the same number in 34 games. On March 11, 1990, Sather unloaded Shtalenkov on the Phoenix Coyotes for a fifth-round draft pick. Nine days later, Sather traded perennial underachiever Mats Lindgren to the New York Islanders for goaltender Tommy Salo, the Swedish phenom who had stoned Team Canada in the 1994 Olympics and won the gold medal for his team.

It wasn't Sather's only move that day. He also shipped Boris Mironov, Dean McAmmond and Jonas Elofsson to the Chicago Blackhawks for Ethan Moreau, Christian Laflamme, Chad Kilger and Dan Cleary. Despite the additions, the Oilers had already lost captain Kelly Buchberger to the Atlanta Thrashers. In addition, Sather dealt Andrei Kovalenko to Philadelphia in exchange for former Ottawa Senators first-round draft pick Alexandre Daigle. Sather had no actual interest in Daigle, who had never lived up to his potential, so traded the forward to Tampa Bay that same day in return for forward Alexander Selivanov.

Although they again crept into the playoffs as the eighth seeded team, there was no Cinderella story for this year's Oilers. Dallas was merciless in its first-round rout of the reshaped team, sweeping the series in four straight games. Each match was decided by only one goal, but the

Oilers team that took to the ice had little time to gel as a unit before the playoffs began.

The playoff series spelled the end of Ron Low's coaching career in Edmonton when the team offered him a new contract for the same salary. Low declined the offer, essentially ceding the job to Kevin Lowe, who had worked the previous season as an assistant coach with the team. The promotion seemed fitting in light of the previous spring's announcement that Wayne Gretzky would retire. Gretzky finished his career as a Ranger and returned to Skyreach Centre in October 1999 to have his number lifted to the rafters of the arena. His famous number 99 was only the second number ever retired by the organization—the first had been Al Hamilton's number 3.

Lowe's team was relatively unchanged from the unit that had been bounced from the playoffs the previous spring. They did, however, have more time to gel during the off-season and in training camp. Doug Weight (21), Ryan Smyth (28), Alexander Selivanov (27) and Bill Guerin (24) all managed to score more than 20 goals, with Weight leading the team in scoring with 72 points. Roman Hamrlik was now the stalwart of the Oilers defence but was joined by draft pick Tom Poti as a potent offensive weapon. Hamrlik finished the year with 45 points while Poti managed 35. Tommy Salo played 70 games for the Oilers, winning 27 and posting a stellar 2.33 GAA. The Oilers again dipped into their past to shore up their netminding, bringing Bill Ranford on board as Salo's backup.

Although far from spectacular, the 1999–2000 version of the Oilers was a consistent, speedy team that could play with the best teams in the league, despite what their 32–34–16–8 record showed (the NHL was now recording overtime losses separately from regular season losses). Again Edmonton tiptoed into the playoffs, this time as the seventh seed, and once more they faced the Dallas Stars. And this year, like in the three years past, the Dallas Stars showed the hockey world that the Oilers were not ready to play at a high enough level to win. Edmonton won game three by a score of 5–2, but Dallas won the other four games to dust the Oilers off in five.

When the Oilers ownership group presented Sather with his annual budget—still well below the league average—in the off-season, he promptly informed the board that he would not be returning for another year as general manager. He flew off to New York to play general manager with one of the league's biggest payrolls, and Kevin Lowe, who had coached the Oilers for only one season, took his place. Continuing in the Oilers' tradition of never letting a former

Oiler fade into retirement, Lowe hired Craig MacTavish as the Oilers' new head coach.

In June, Lowe traded Roman Hamrlik to the New York Islanders for promising defenceman Eric Brewer. With Bill Guerin's contract due to expire at the end of the 2000–01 hockey season and the forward likely to demand more money than the Oilers could afford, Lowe traded him to Boston in exchange for Anson Carter and a draft pick. Carter was a capable fit in the Oilers' roster, scoring 16 goals and 26 assists in 61 games. Weight led the team in scoring with 90 points while Ryan Smyth eclipsed the 30-goal plateau for the first time since his rookie season. Mike Grier added another 20, and Janne Niinimaa led all defencemen with 46 points. The season also saw the debut of another Oilers draft prospect, Mike Comrie, a local product who played in 41 games in 2000–01 and managed to score 22 points. Salo won 36 of 73 games, posting a 2.46 GAA and a .904 save percentage. The Oilers finished with a record of 39–28–12–3, their first winning record in years.

Their ongoing string of playoff appearances against Dallas, however, was turning into a curse that was becoming less funny every year. The two teams squared off again in the first round, but the Oilers still couldn't find a way to beat the Green Machine from Texas. The teams traded victories in the first two games, Dallas winning game one 2–1 and the Oilers game two 4–3. Dallas edged the Oilers 3–2 in game three, but the Oilers came back and won game four 2–1. The two victories were the best the Oilers could do. Dallas won games five and six 4–3 and 3–1. It was by far the closest series of the last four the two teams had played, but the Oilers were tired of close.

The end of the season brought bad news for the team and its fans. The issue of finances again reared its ugly head as Lowe tried his best to field a competitive team on such a tiny payroll. Doug Weight had only one year left on his contract, and Lowe knew there was no chance the Oilers could afford him. In an age where any player's first loyalty was proving to be increasingly to the bank instead of the team that let him play, Lowe had no choice but trade him. In the off-season, Lowe unloaded Weight and Michel Riesen on the St. Louis Blues for Marty Reasoner, Jochen Hecht and Jan Horacek.

Trading their captain and leading scorer for the last five years had a disastrous effect on the squad. Although other players tried to step in to fill the void left by Weight's absence and the team fought to another superb record, it would not be enough. In 2001–02, the Oilers again missed the playoffs.

Chapter Nine

Fighting Back

In any other NHL season, a total of 92 points would be enough to guarantee a high play-off seed. In the 2001–02 season, the total wasn't even enough to guarantee a playoff spot.

The Oilers continued their strong play from the previous season, despite the loss of team leader Doug Weight. Jason "Gator" Smith, one of the Oilers' hard-hitting rocks on defence, inherited the title of captain and took the helm of a young team full of talent but short on experience. After a respectable debut, second-year forward Mike Comrie led the Oilers in scoring with 33 goals and 27 assists. Anson Carter also proved he was capable of filling at least one of Doug Weight's shoes, scoring 28 goals and adding 32 assists. Although his season was shortened by 20 games due to injury, Ryan Smyth also chipped in 15 goals of his own.

Some of the members of the team were not playing up to the level the fans were expecting, and they quickly turned on Tom Poti for his lacklustre play and frequent defensive gaffs. Lowe eventually traded him to the New York Rangers along with Rem Murray, for forward Mike York and a fourth-round pick in the upcoming draft.

Tommy Salo started the season well for the Oilers but began to slump after a heartbreaking experience in the 2002 Salt Lake City Olympics in which he flinched on what should have been a routine save, costing the Swedes a potential berth in the gold medal game. Team Canada members Ryan Smyth and Eric Brewer went on to win gold, and Salo was quickly vilified by his fans back in Sweden. Although his 2.22 GAA was the lowest ever for an Oilers starting goaltender, his 30–28–10 record was only two games above .500.

The Oilers' 92 points was still not good enough to qualify for the playoffs, and the coming offseason brought more tweaks to the lineup. On June 22 Lowe traded Jochen Hecht, who had scored 16 goals and 24 assists as an Oiler, to Buffalo to bolster the team's position in the upcoming draft. Now with two second-round picks, Lowe drafted Chicoutimi Sagueneens goaltender Jeff Deslauriers with the 31st pick then selected Kootenay Ice centre Jarret Stoll with the 36th pick. In 47 games the previous season, Stoll had scored 32 goals and 34 assists. The Oilers used their third pick in the second round to take bruising defenceman Matt Greene from the Green Bay Gamblers.

The 2002–03 season was full of obstacles for the Oilers because both Ryan Smyth and Mike Comrie missed games due to injury. Although his numbers were respectable—29 wins in 65 starts with a 2.71 GAA—Tommy Salo seemed to have lost the ability to make the big save that the Oilers had grown to count on. Rumours continued to swirl that there was some sort of conflict with a teammate that was affecting Salo on a personal level. Ryan Smyth led the team in scoring with 27 goals and 34 assists, while speedy centre Todd Marchant overcame his reputation for having fast feet and slow hands by scoring 20 goals and assisting on 40 others. Mike Comrie's production slipped to 20 goals in 69 games, but Anson Carter's 25 goals and Mike York's 22 markers made up for the shortfall. In the end, the Oilers finished the season with a 36–26–11–9 record, good enough to sneak into the playoffs they had been shut out of the previous year. Carter's excellent numbers, however, further increased his market value. Lowe knew he would ultimately lose the winger at the end of the year, the last year of his contract. Continuing in the Oilers' tradition of trading away quality players with big price tags,

Lowe dealt Carter and prospect Ales Pisa to the New York Rangers for defenceman Cory Cross and forward Radek Dvorak on March 11. Lowe also sent Niinimaa to the Islanders in exchange for wingers Brad Isbister and Raffi Torres.

Even though they'd had one summer away from the post-season, the Oilers could do nothing to shake the Dallas Stars from what seemed to be a perennial springtime match-up. This year's series went to six games, but the Oilers just weren't strong enough to handle the fast, physical Stars. The Oilers won game one 2–1 and game three 3–2 but dropped game two to Dallas by a 6–1 margin. The team managed only five more goals over the next three games, ultimately losing the series on Dallas' home ice.

The end of the season also meant the end of a career for another promising young Oiler. Native son Mike Comrie started the season by holding out. Rumours continued to find fodder on the Internet, intimating that Comrie had something to do with Tommy Salo's notably poorer play over the last season. Lowe promptly shipped Comrie to Philadelphia for prospect defenceman Jeff Woywitka and a first-round pick in the 2004 draft. When Comrie returned to Edmonton to play his first game as a Flyer, the rumours seemed to hold true as fans held up any number of disparaging signs.

"Players, lock up your wives," read one.

As if Comrie and Salo were perpetually linked somehow, Lowe also traded Salo to the Colorado Avalanche at the trade deadline, handing the starting netminding duties to young American Ty Conklin and to Finnish backup Jussi Markkanen.

Before there were trades, however, there was THE GAME. In a public relations stunt the NHL had never seen before, the Edmonton Oilers announced in the off-season that the team would play one of its regular season games outdoors. The game against the Montréal Canadiens was dubbed the Heritage Hockey Classic and would be played on an outdoor rink built at Commonwealth Stadium, home to Edmonton's CFL Eskimos. More thrilling still, the team announced the actual game would be preceded by an oldtimers game between the Oilers and Habs alumni of the 1980s. The alumni Oilers beat the Canadiens 2–0, but the modern-day Oilers could not repeat the performance. The Canadiens beat the Oilers 4–3 under the lights of Commonwealth Stadium.

What should have been a source of inspiration for the Oilers turned into the exact opposite as the team managed only five wins over the course of the next 20 games. The Heritage Classic was actually the start of a six-game winless streak that seemed to stretch on forever. So often the Oilers took a lead into the third period before surrendering a tie or a loss altogether. Lowe pulled off another trade in March, acquiring proven sniper Petr Nedved from the New York Rangers for a pair of prospects and a draft pick, but even Nedved couldn't do much. The Oilers' 36–29–12–5 record was still good but not good enough for the playoffs. Their post-season fate was sealed on April 3, 2004, when the team dropped its last game of the season, a game they absolutely had to win, 5–2 to the Vancouver Canucks. There would be no post-season hockey in Edmonton that summer. Instead, Oilers fans jumped on the Flames bandwagon and cheered on their southern Alberta rivals as the Flames made a potent charge for the Stanley Cup. Although they were the first Canadian team since the 1994 Vancouver Canucks to make the final, they could not beat the Tampa Bay Lightning, who won hockey's Holy Grail.

As unappetizing as watching a team based out of Florida win the Stanley Cup was, what followed during the summer was downright nauseating. The collective bargaining agreement between the NHL and NHLPA had expired, and there was absolutely no reason to expect the two sides to negotiate a new one before the start of the 2004–05 season. NHL commissioner Gary Bettman was fighting for small-market teams such as the Oilers, trying to guarantee "cost certainty" for teams playing in smaller cities. He was after a cap for escalating player salaries and "linkage," a formula that placed a limit on what percentage of its revenues a team could spend on its payroll. The agreement that had ended the 1994–95 lockout was viewed by many as the catalyst for the explosion in players' salaries and the decline of the playing power of the small-market team. There was no way Bettman and the owners were going to cave to the union this time around. On September 29, the NHL announced the regular season would not start in October.

The cost was high. Although both sides traded a few proposals, neither would budge. The players offered a 24-percent salary rollback, but the NHL wouldn't entertain any new agreement that did not somehow limit how much each team could spend on salaries. More than 350 players decided to play in Europe, and the players who remained behind started publicly dissenting from the union line, saying they would play under a salary cap if it was fair to both sides. Despite a flurry of eleventh-hour meetings, some of which took place at airports, neither side could broker an agreement that was acceptable to the other. On February 16, in a move the likes of which no professional sport had ever seen, Bettman announced the cancellation of the entire season.

Just when the NHL started talking about using replacement players in the upcoming season and the media started to speculate that another season could be cancelled, the union broke. Between July 21 and 22, the NHL board of governors and the NHLPA voted to ratify a new agreement, which included a salary cap with upper and lower ends, as well as linkage. Knowing the cancelled season had turned many fans off the game, especially those south of the border, Bettman also announced several rule changes that were designed to make the game more entertaining. Two-line passes would now be allowed. Any tie game that wasn't settled after a five-minute overtime period would be settled by a shootout, except in the playoffs. The league imposed limits on the ever-ballooning size of goaltending equipment, as well as reaffirmed its commitment to cracking down on the obstruction style of play that was dragging down speedy teams like the Edmonton Oilers. The league reintroduced tag-up offsides and moved the goal nets two feet closer to the end boards. Lastly, the NHL created an area on either side of the goal in which goaltenders were no longer able to handle the puck.

The salary cap, combined with a revenue-sharing scheme in which the top-10 moneymaking teams contributed to a fund split by the 15 lowest money-making teams, was good news for the Oilers. Having been forced to trade off the likes of Doug Weight and Anson Carter because they made too much money, the team could now start using the new mechanisms to start paying competitive players a competitive salary.

Kevin Lowe took his new budget and started shopping around. What he found would generate one of the most memorable teams in recent Oilers' history—for the entire one season that it lasted.

Chapter Ten

One Wild Ride

No one in Edmonton could believe it at first. Everyone knew that the new, fiscally equal NHL was going to open up avenues for the Edmonton Oilers but no one, NO ONE expected this.

It was a viciously hot August day in Edmonton when Kevin Lowe made the announcement. Sadly, he had decided it was time to part with young gold medal–winning defenceman Eric Brewer and prospects Doug Lynch and Jeff Woywitka.

What the Oilers would get in return no one could have predicted. Chris Pronger was one of the most dominant players in the league, a towering six-foot-six defenceman with a booming slapshot and 210 pounds he had no compunction throwing around. He had played his entire career to date—with the exception of his first two seasons—with the St. Louis Blues. He had

won both the Norris Trophy as the league's top
defenceman and the Hart Trophy as the league's
MVP in 1999, as well as a gold medal when he
played on Canada's Salt Lake City Olympic team
in 2002.

Lowe's second announcement seemed just as
incredible as the first. The furor from the Pronger
trade had barely faded when he announced he
had traded Mike York and a conditional draft pick
to the New York Islanders for Michael Peca. The
centreman was known as a solid two-way player,
a forward with defensive abilities and a nose for
the net, who had twice won the Selke trophy
as the league's best defensive forward. He had,
four times in his career, scored 20 goals or more.
He had also been a member of the gold medal–
winning team in Salt Lake City.

With the defence effectively shored up and
Peca being touted as a potential first-line centre,
the biggest question remained goaltending. Ty
Conklin and Jussi Markkanen were due to battle
it out for the starting job. Neither, however, had
made a decisive play for the role, and the Oilers
coaching and management staff spent the rest
of the season perpetually answering questions
about the state of the team's netminding.

The new-look Oilers seemed solid right
down the middle. Centres Shawn Horcoff and
Jarrett Stoll backed up Peca on the other lines,

while Ryan Smyth, dodgy winger Alex Hemsky and local product Fernando Pisani covered the wings. Ethan Moreau was there to kill penalties, and Georges Laraques was ready to punish any opponent who stepped out of line.

The Oilers won their first game against Colorado, 4–3, on home ice. They beat Vancouver three nights later in their first shootout under the league's new rules then doubled up Anaheim 4–2. The three-game winning streak quickly dissolved as the Oilers proceeded to lose their next seven games in a row, two of which came at Calgary's hands. A pair of five-game winning streaks, one in November and one in December, arrested the damage the slide had caused, but the team was already starting to make some changes to address the team's possible shortcomings.

When Ty Conklin went down with an injury, he was replaced on the bench by prospect Mike Morrison, who ended up starting 25 games, winning 11 of them. He also became known for his prowess in the shootout, as the Oilers won five straight shootout games in which he played. MacTavish even experimented with bringing the rookie into the game only for the shootout, but Morrison was often too "cold" to be effective.

Conklin was eventually placed on waivers, having started 18 games and winning only eight, but no one claimed him. Markkanen shouldered the rest of the load for much of the season, winning 15 of 37 starts and posting a 3.13 GAA.

The goaltenders were not to blame for the Oilers' on-again, off-again performance in 2005–06. Although Chris Pronger and Steve Staios were adequately patrolling the blueline, the rest of the defensive corps wasn't playing up to the same level. Determined to correct the situation, Lowe traded prospect Tony Salmelainen to the Chicago Blackhawks on January 26 for defenceman Jaroslav Spacek. On the same day, Lowe traded perennial underachiever Jani Rita and defenceman Cory Cross to Pittsburgh for proven puck-mover Dick Tarnstrom.

Lowe still needed to address the goaltending issue. His three-goalie rotation wasn't helping the team or the goaltenders themselves. On March 8, 2006, Lowe dealt a first-round draft pick and a conditional third-round pick to the Minnesota Wild for keeper Dwayne Roloson. The 36-year-old had been splitting the puck-stopping duties with Manny Fernandez in Minnesota since 2001–02. When Fernandez signed a new contract during the 2005–06 season, Roloson knew he was going to be relegated to the backup role.

One day after trading for Roloson, Lowe decided to add a little offensive jump to the team as well by trading Marty Reasoner and prospect

Yan Stastny to the Boston Bruins for forward Sergei Samsonov. The Russian winger had scored 20 or more goals four times since his 1997 rookie year but had been hampered in recent years by injuries.

The trades didn't seem to have any tangible effect on the Oilers. They lost 11 of their final 20 games of the season, squeaking into the playoffs as the eighth seed only as a result of a 2–1 win against the Anaheim Mighty Ducks in the team's second-last game of the season.

For the first time in almost eight years, the Oilers first opponent was not the Dallas Stars. As the eighth seed, the Oilers drew the Detroit Red Wings as their first-round opponent, and the series opened in earnest on April 21, 2006. Going into the game, the Oilers were picked by some oddsmakers as anywhere from 40–1 to 75–1 shots at winning the Stanley Cup. The series-opening game seemed to bear those predictions out. Although Sergei Samsonov scored one goal and assisted on Chris Pronger's goal in the second period, the Red Wings tied that game at two in the third, sending the game into overtime. Less than three minutes into the second overtime frame, Kirk Maltby scored, winning it for the Red Wings.

The Oilers came into game two with a new attitude and a new approach. Dedicated Edmonton fans and media watched, somewhat perplexed by both the appearance of rookie Brad Winchester in the lineup and the Oilers' use of the neutral zone trap to slow down the Red Wings' swift attack. Both turned out to be judicious moves because the Red Wings scored only twice, and Winchester scored the game-winning goal at the 18:46 mark of the second period.

"A coach has to be right occasionally," said MacTavish after the game.

At first it looked as though the Oilers had lost game three. The game was tied 3–3 going into overtime, and the entire hockey nation seemed to collectively turn off their TVs in disgust when it appeared that Jason Williams had scored the winning goal for Detroit. A video review, however, showed that the puck had actually slid underneath the point at which the net met the ice. Williams was not the hero after all. Jarrett Stoll, who scored the winning goal at 8:45 of the second overtime period was, and the fans showed their approval. Game three proved to be the catalyst of the dedicated following the Oilers would attract in the weeks to come.

"We needed that win, and we needed it bad," said Stoll afterwards.

The Red Wings needed to win game four, and they did, riding three powerplay goals to a 4–2 win to even the series at two games a piece.

Edmonton was ready to prove that the team was prepared to do whatever it took to win.

In game five of the series, Shawn Horcoff showed he was completely committed to the Oilers' playoff run when he decided to dive head-first into a Nicklas Lidstrom slapshot to preserve the team's lead. Chris Pronger was the Oilers' quarterback, assisting on all three Edmonton goals as Edmonton won game five, pushing the Wings to the brink of elimination.

And for most of game six, it looked as if the series was heading back to Detroit for game seven. The Wings built up a 2–0 lead heading into the third period. Then the Oilers came alive. Fernando Pisani scored his fourth and fifth goals of the playoffs to tie the game, only to watch Detroit score at the 10-minute mark to leap ahead by one. Rather than sit back and accept defeat, the Oilers seemed to collectively decide to win the series on home ice. Alex Hemsky scored twice in less than three minutes, with one goal standing up under video review, to cement a 4–3 win for Edmonton. Rexall Place, as Northlands Coliseum was now known, practically exploded.

"I haven't seen anything like that. The place erupted. It was unbelievable," said Roloson.

As the eighth playoff seed, the Oilers were destined never to start a series at home in the

2005–06 playoffs. Their next opponent was the San Jose Sharks, whose lineup was dotted with solid, gifted players such as forwards Joe Thornton and Patrick Marleau, and Jonathan Cheechoo, who had scored the most goals of any player in the NHL during the regular season. Vesa Toskala had taken over the starting goaltending position from veteran Evgeni Nabokov in the first round.

Rather than rely on their speed and skill, however, the Sharks came out and literally started pounding the Oilers to the ice in game one. The physical confrontation knocked Edmonton back on their heels, so much so that the team managed only two shots on goal in the second period and five in the third. Spacek scored on one of nine shots in the first period to open the scoring, but San Jose tied the game five minutes later, then scored one more in the second to win the first game 2–1. Roloson was solid, turning aside 30 shots compared to the Oilers' 16, but the rest of the squad seemed tentative in the wake of the Sharks onslaught.

"They're a fast, big, physical team. If anything, after tonight, we realize how much we're going to have to bring in order win the series," said Peca.

Edmonton steeled itself in game two and met the Sharks' body play head-on, adding Georges Laraques and big defenceman Matt Green to the lineup. They even managed 25 shots on Toskala, but the Sharks piled 38 on Roloson. Joe Thornton broke open a 1–1 game with a goal in the second period with his first of the playoffs to give the Sharks another 2–1 victory.

In Edmonton, the CBC crews were measuring the crowd noise in decibels and comparing the total volume inside Rexall Place to jet aircraft and gunfire. Buoyed by their fans, the Oilers clenched down defensively, holding San Jose to two shots on net in the first period. Marc-Andre Bergeron scored on the powerplay in the first period, but the Sharks responded with two in the second to take a 2–1 lead. With seven minutes left in the third period, Raffi Torres tied the game.

It was the Oilers' heart and soul, Ryan Smyth, who eventually set the tone for the rest of the series and the game. The crowd watched in horror as a Chris Pronger clearing attempt caught Smyth in the mouth, spewing blood and teeth all over the ice. Minutes after the incident, however, Smyth was back on the ice. In the third overtime period, Smyth grabbed the puck behind the net and tried to score on the wraparound. Toskala stopped him, but the rebound went to Shawn Horcoff, who bulged the twine and sent a tired but enraptured Rexall Place into a frenzy.

Smyth's gritty determination in the face of pain proved to be the catalyst for the Oilers for the rest of the series. On May 12, they came back from a 2–0 deficit to win game three 6–3, chasing Toskala from the net in the third period in favour of Nabokov.

"Now we have an opportunity to take a stranglehold on the series in the next game," said MacTavish. "The first to win in the opponent's building will probably win the series."

It was the Oilers that managed to accomplish the feat. Despite getting only 18 shots on goal in game five, the Oilers scored six, two of which belonged to Fernando Pisani, to win the game 6–3. Three of the goals came on the powerplay as Edmonton's special teams finally started to click.

With the offence finally producing, Roloson sat back in his net in game six and decided to win one for his team. He turned aside 24 shots, 12 in the first period, to post his first shutout of the post-season and lead the Oilers to not just a game six victory but also a berth in the Stanley Cup semifinal.

"We just outworked them. They just seemed to have a lot of guys who weren't committed to making the extra effort at times. That was the difference," said Peca after the game.

The Oilers returned to California for the Western Conference final, this time against the Mighty Ducks of Anaheim. As if now convinced he could do more than just stop the puck, Roloson decided to get things started for Edmonton in the first period. With Chris Pronger in the penalty box for elbowing at the 18-minute mark of the first period, Roloson got his goal stick on a lazy dump-in by the Ducks, put it on his back hand and shovelled a high, arcing pass to a streaking Michael Peca. Peca faked Ducks goalie Ilya Bryzgalov, pulled it to his backhand and slipped it into the net to give the team a 1–0 lead. Alex Hemsky and Todd Harvey would each add one more to give the Oilers a 3–1 win in game one.

"Once he turned his hand over, I knew I had to get up ice," said Peca afterwards.

"I used to do it in college all the time," said Roloson.

Even though they sported talented forwards such as Teemu Selanne and Joffrey Lupul, as well as stalwart defenceman Scott Neidermayer, the Ducks seemed unable to cope with the Oilers' breakneck style of play. Pisani scored his playoff-leading eighth goal in the second period of game two to break a 1–1 tie, propelling Edmonton to another 3–1 victory.

Game three proved to be more exciting than it should have been. The night saw Oilers long-time anthem singer Paul Lorieau start a playoff tradition by holding his microphone aloft and letting the crowd finish the national anthem. The Oilers scored four goals in the first 25 minutes of the game, three alone in a 2:21 span in the second period to build up a 4–0 lead. It proved to be barely good enough, however, as the Ducks scored four goals in the third period. Fortunately for the Oilers, Pisani scored his ninth of the playoffs before Selanne scored the Ducks' fourth goal, giving Edmonton a wild 5–4 win.

"At no point was I comfortable at 4–0 because I knew the energy level of our team. It was a wild game we feel fortunate to have won," said Mac-Tavish.

It was only because of the flu that the Ducks won game three. The bug ran rampant through the Oilers locker room, infecting a handful of core players, including Roloson, who threw up between periods. The weakened Oilers still managed to score 3 goals on 23 shots, but Anaheim poured 46 on Roloson, scoring on 6 for a 6–3 win.

Two nights later, feeling rested and a little better than they had the previous game, the Oilers posted a 2–1 win to achieve what no one in the NHL predicted at the start of the post-season.

The Oilers were going to play in the Stanley Cup final.

"You talk about this all the time, but until it really happens it's a dream," said Horcoff.

Game one against the Carolina Hurricanes was at once thrilling and devastating. Pisani banged home a rebound to continue his frenetic scoring pace and give the Oilers a 1–0 lead. At the 10-minute mark of the second period, Pronger was awarded the first-ever penalty shot in Stanley Cup final history when Hurricanes defenceman Niclas Wallin closed his hand on the puck in the crease. His ensuing goal was followed six minutes later by an Ethan Moreau wrist shot to give the Oilers a 3–0 lead.

The three-goal lead was not good enough. The Hurricanes scored their first goal in the second period, then scored three more times to take a 4–3 lead. Alex Hemsky roofed a backhander past Ward late in the third to tie the game. And then it happened.

With six minutes remaining, Oilers defenceman Marc-Andre Bergeron piled Hurricanes forward Andrew Laad into Roloson. Laad came down hard on Roloson so hard that the collision tore apart his knee, sidelining him for the remainder of the playoffs. Ty Conklin, dressed as the backup, took over in net then coughed up a blind backhand pass to Rod Brind'Amour with only 31 seconds remaining. It would have taken more effort for Brind'Amour not to score, but of course he didn't do that. The Hurricanes took game one 5–4.

Predictably, Jussi Markkanen got the start in game two over Conklin, but the Oilers' effort level that night ranked between barely detectable and totally invisible. Edmonton spent most of the night in the penalty box, giving up three powerplay goals on 10 opportunities to help Carolina win game two 5–0.

"That's inexcusable. There's no reason for us to take as many penalties as we did," said Peca. "We're making ourselves look bad, and we're leaving our goalie out to dry.

Returning home to Edmonton turned out to be good for the Oilers. Not even three minutes into the game, Horcoff got a stick on a Spacek one-timer to open the scoring. Brind'Amour banged home his own rebound in the third to tie the game, but Ryan Smyth crashed the net on a give-and-go with Alex Hemsky, knocking in the winning goal that stood up on video review.

Game four was not as kind as previous game fours had been to Edmonton. Despite playing on home ice, the Oilers went 0-for-5 on the powerplay in a defensive slugfest that featured a grand total of 41 shots on goal by both teams. Cory Stillman blasted home a one-timer in the first period to nullify Samsonov's fourth goal of the playoffs. He then assisted on the winning goal in the second period to give the Hurricanes a 3–1 stranglehold on the series.

Just as the Oilers gave away game one, the Hurricanes give away game five. With the game tied 3–3 in the first overtime period and with Steve Staios in the penalty box for tripping, Pisani snagged a lazy clearing pass by Cory Stillman, walked in on Cam Ward and fired a shot right under the crossbar to win the game 4–3. The goal was Pisani's second of the game and his 12th of the playoffs.

"The pass was coming so slow so that's why I jumped up," he said after the game. "I was in the right place at the right time."

Game six was as perfect a game as the Oilers played all year. Markkanen turned away a paltry 16 shots while Edmonton scored three power-play goals en route to a 4–0 win. Pisani scored his 13th on a backhand deflecting off defender Glenn Wesley. Raffi Torres tipped home a Steve Staios slapshot in the second while Ryan Smyth powered a backhander over Ward in the third. Horcoff sealed the game with his seventh on a low snapper that sneaked past Ward's glove.

The series was tied at 3–3. The Stanley Cup would be won the very next game.

"I think we've got them right where we want them," said Torres.

That confidence lasted less than two minutes into game seven when Aaron Ward slipped a shot past a screened Jussi Markkanen to put Carolina up 1–0. Frantisek Kaberle doubled the their lead on a point shot that deflected off Jason Smith. Pisani stepped up for the Oilers again, scoring his 14th by knocking in a Rem Murray rebound barely one minute into the third to give the thousands of Oilers fans in Edmonton and in Canada some semblance of hope that this most unlikely of playoff runs wasn't over.

MacTavish called Markkanen to the bench during the final two minutes for the extra attacker, but Jason Williams got a stick on the puck and punched it into the empty net, dashing the hopes of an Edmonton team that had played with more heart and determination than any Stanley Cup contender in recent history.

"I don't even know if there are words to describe it," said Peca. "We knew we were defying the odds each and every time we won a game, every time we won a series. We wanted to rewrite history."

"It sucked," said Pisani of the loss.

The loss was crushing for both the team and its fans back home in Edmonton. Yet once the bitter sensation of defeat wore off, there was hope again in the capital city. After all, if this team could come so far so fast in the post-season, surely they'd contend again next year.

It started as a rumour, but the second the rumour was picked up by the media, it began to dawn on most Edmontonians that it was more than likely true. The day before the NHL entry draft, TSN reported that Chris Pronger had asked for a trade to another city for "personal reasons."

Pronger never said exactly what those personal reasons were. The media speculated his wife Loren was unhappy in Edmonton and had in fact spent most of the season in St. Louis. In the absence of any concrete explanation, the Oilers fans unleashed their fury on the departing defenceman. Rumours circulated on the Oilers website bulletin board that Pronger had had an affair with a local newscaster. The rumour churned so loudly that the Oilers webmaster threatened to shut down the bulletin board if people didn't stop talking about it.

Pronger, however, never explained himself.

"People want to make up stuff? I'll go with that. If they want to make it up about me, that's fine. But if you start bringing in my family, you're starting to get a little close."

Ten days after Pronger's request for a trade, Kevin Lowe granted his wish on July 3 and traded him to the Anaheim Mighty Ducks for forward Joffrey Lupul, defensive prospect Ladislav Smid, Anaheim's 2007 first-round draft pick, a conditional first-round draft pick, and Anaheim's 2008 second-round draft pick.

The bleeding didn't stop there. In mid-July, Michael Peca, who had joined the Oilers mere hours after Pronger, signed a one-year deal with the Leafs. Edmonton also watched Georges Laraques, one of the city's most beloved players, sign a deal with the Coyotes, and Jaroslav Spacek decided to sign with the Sabres. All four moves came within days of one another, leaving most of the city dazed and a little confused about what exactly they could expect from the team next year.

Some good news came in the middle of all the bad. Dwayne Roloson quickly agreed to a three-year, $11 million contract, while centre Shawn Horcoff signed off on a three-year, $10.8 million contract. On August 11, the team also announced they had signed two-time 30-goal scorer Petr Sykora to a one-year deal.

The fringes might have changed, but for the time being it appears that the core of the Oilers team— Ryan Smyth, Shawn Horcoff, Jarrett Stoll, Steve Staios, Fernando Pisani and Alex Hemsky—are content to start over.

In Edmonton, it's always been this way.

APPENDIX I

The Stats

Legend	
GP – Games Played	GF – Goals For
W – Wins	GA – Goals Against
L – Loses	Pts – Points
T – Ties	PIM – Penalty in Minutes
OT – Overtime	

Scoring Leaders

Player	Games Played	Goals	Assists	Points
Wayne Gretzky	696	583	1086	1669
Jari Kurri	754	474	596	1043
Mark Messier	851	392	642	1034
Glenn Anderson	845	417	489	906
Paul Coffey	532	209	460	669
Doug Weight	588	157	420	577
Ryan Smyth	761	249	274	523
Esa Tikkanen	490	178	258	436
Kevin Lowe	1037	74	309	383
Charlie Huddy	694	61	287	368

Season by Season Record in the National Hockey League

Season	GP	W	L	T	OTL	GF	GA	Points
WHL								
1972–73	78	37	35	6	N/A	259	250	80
1973–74	78	44	321	2	N/A	332	275	90
1974–75	78	36	38	4	N/A	279	279	76
1975–76	81	27	49	5	N/A	268	345	59
1976-77	81	34	43	4	N/A	243	304	72
1977–78	80	38	39	3	N/A	309	307	79
1978–79	80	48	30	2	N/A	340	266	98
NHL								
1979–80	80	28	39	13	N/A	301	322	69
1980–81	80	29	35	16	N/A	328	327	74
1981–82	80	48	17	15	N/A	417	295	111
1982–83	80	47	21	12	N/A	424	315	106
1983–84	80	57	18	5	N/A	446	314	119
1984–85	80	49	20	11	N/A	401	298	109
1985–86	80	56	17	7	N/A	426	310	119
1986–87	80	50	24	6	N/A	372	284	106
1987–88	80	44	25	11	N/A	363	288	99
1988–89	80	38	34	8	N/A	325	306	84
1989–90	80	38	28	14	N/A	315	283	90
1990–91	80	37	37	4	N/A	272	272	80
1991–92	80	36	34	10	N/A	295	297	82
1992–93	84	26	50	8	N/A	242	337	60
1993–94	84	25	45	14	N/A	261	305	64
1994–95	48	17	27	4	N/A	136	183	38
1995–96	82	30	44	8	N/A	240	304	68
1996–97	82	36	37	9	N/A	252	247	81
1997–98	82	35	37	10	N/A	215	224	80
1998–99	82	33	37	12	N/A	230	226	78
1999-2000	82	32	26	16	8	226	212	88
2000–01	82	39	28	12	3	243	222	93
2001–02	82	38	28	12	4	205	182	92
2002–03	82	36	26	11	9	231	230	92
2003–04	82	36	29	12	5	221	208	89
2004–05	Season Cancelled by Lockout							
2005–06	82	41	28	N/A	13	256	251	95

Season and Playoff Record

Season	Regular Season Finish	Playoffs
WHL		
1972–73	Fourth, West	Did not qualify
1973–74	Third, West	Lost Preliminary Round
1974–75	Fifth, Canadian	Did not qualify
1975–76	Fourth, Canadian	Lost quarterfinal
1976-77	Fourth, West	Lost quarterfinal
1977–78	Fifth, WHA	Lost Preliminary Round
1978–79	Fifth, WHA	Lost Avco Cup to Winnipeg
NHL		
1979–80	Fourth, Smythe Division	Lost in preliminary round
1980–81	Fourth, Smythe Division	Lost Quarterfinal
1981–82	First, Smythe Division	Lost Division Semifinal
1982–83	First, Smythe Division	Lost Stanley Cup Final vs. New York Islanders
1983–84	First, Smythe Division	Won Stanley Cup vs. New York Islanders
1984–85	First, Smythe Division	Won Stanley Cup vs. Philadelphia Flyers
1985–86	First, Smythe Division	Lost Division Final
1986–87	First, Smythe Division	Won Stanley Cup vs. Philadelphia Flyers
1987–88	Second, Smythe Division	Won Stanley Cup vs. Boston Bruins
1988–89	Third, Smythe Division	Lost Conference Semifinal
1989–90	Second, Smythe Division	Won Stanley Cup vs. Boston Bruins
1990–91	Third, Smythe Division	Lost Conference Final
1991–92	Third, Smythe Division	Lost Conference Final
1992–93	Fifth, Smythe Division	Did not qualify
1993–94	Sixth, Pacific	Did not qualify
1994–95	Fifth, Pacific	Did not qualify
1995–96	Fifth, Pacific	Did not qualify
1996–97	Third, Pacific	Lost Conference Semfinal
1997–98	Third, Pacific	Lost Conference Semfinal
1998–99	Second, Northwest	Lost Conference Quarterfinal
1999-2000	Second, Northwest	Lost Conference Quarterfinal
2000–01	Second, Northwest	Lost Conference Quarterfinal
2001–02	Third, Northwest	Did not qualify
2002–03	Fourth, Northwest	Lost Conference Quarterfinal
2003–04	Fourth, Northwest	Did not qualify
2004–05	Season Cancelled by Lockout	
2005-06	Third, Northwest	Lost Stanley Cup Final vs. Carolina

Notes on Sources

Boer, Peter. *Weird Facts About Canadian Hockey*. Montréal: Overtime Books, 2005.

Barret, Tom, et al. *What a Wild Ride!* Edmonton: *The Edmonton Journal*, 2006.

Edmonton Oilers. *Edmonton Oilers Official Guide*. Edmonton: Edmonton Oilers, 2005.

Gaschnitz, Michael. *The Edmonton Oilers*. Jefferson: McFarland & Co., 2003.

Gzowski, Peter. *The Game of Our Lives*. Surrey: Heritage House, 1981.

Hunter, Douglas. *The Glory Barons: The Saga of the Edmonton Oilers*. Toronto: Viking, 1999.

Jones, Terry. *Edmonton's Hockey Knights: 79 to 99*. Edmonton: *The Edmonton Sun*, 1998.

Jones, Terry. *Wayne Gretzky: An Oiler Forever*. Edmonton: *The Edmonton Sun*, 1999.

Lowe, Kevin, et al. *Champions: The Making of the Edmonton Oilers*. Scarborough: Prentice-Hall Canada, 1988.

Poulton, Jay. *Hockey Record Breakers*. Montréal: Overtime Books, 2004.

The Hockey News. *Total Gretzky: The Magic, The Legend, The Numbers*. Toronto: McClelland & Stewart, 1999.

Turchansky, Ray. *Edmonton Oilers Hockey Club: Celebrating 25 Years in the Heartland of Hockey.* Edmonton: The Edmonton Journal Group, 2003.

Heritage Classic: A November to Remember. CBC, 2004.

Web Sources

Edmonton Oilers (n.d.). www.edmontonoilers.com. Retrieved January 1 to August 11, 2006.

The Internet Hockey Database (n.d.). www.hockeydb.com. Retrieved January 1 to August 12, 2006.

The National Hockey League Website. (n.d.) www.nhl.com. Retrieved January 1 to August 12, 2006.

ESPN: The Worldwide Leader in Sports (n.d.). www.espn.go.com. Retrieved April 21, 2006.

CBC Sports Online: Face-off 2004–2005 (n.d.). www.cbc.ca/sports/indepth/cba. Retrieved August 7, 2006.

Peter Boer

Peter Boer has been a consummate hockey fan since his parents first bribed him with a chocolate bar to skate from the red line to the blue line at the age of four. It took him three years to score his first goal, but he never looked back. Since realizing actual talent was a necessary requirement for an NHL career, Peter has immersed himself in the game in other ways. He has refereed and minded the score clock for beer-league hockey, coached women's hockey and been a goal judge, penalty box staff, security guard, ticket taker and blood cleaner for the CIS University of Alberta Golden Bears and Concordia University Stingers.

When he's not spending his Saturday nights bemoaning the current state of the NHL, Peter covers sports, as well as politics and news for the *St. Albert Gazette*. He is the author of five other non-fiction books, including *Weird Facts About Canadian Hockey*. This is his second book for OverTime Books.